Tarot

Reader 2008

Featuring

Ruth Ann and Wald Amberstone, Elizabeth Barrette,
Nina Lee Braden, Dallas Jennifer Cobb, Sally Cragin,
Elizabeth Genco, Mary K. Greer, Magenta Griffith,
Elizabeth Hazel, Annie Jones, Corrine Kenner,
Mark McElroy, Leeda Alleyn Pacotti, Rachel Pollack,
Kevin Quigley, Roslyn Reid, Janina Renée, James Ricklef,
Cerridwen Iris Shea, Valerie Sim, Thalassa,
James Wells, Gail Wood, and Winter Wren

ISBN-10 0-7387-0681-7

ISBN-13 978-0-7387-0681-1

Cover Images: *The Mystic Faerie Tarot* by Linda Ravenscroft

Editing/Design by K. M. Brielmaier
Cover Design by Kevin R. Brown
Interior Art by Adam Dalgarno
Art Direction by Lynne Menturweck

You can order Llewellyn annuals and books from *New Worlds*, Llewellyn's magazine catalog. To request a free copy of the catalog, call toll-free 1-877-NEW-WRLD, or visit http://subscriptions.llewellyn.com.

Table of Contents

The Fool: Tools for the Journey

The Magician: Practical Applications

✳ ☆ ✳ ☆ ✳ ☆ ✳ ☆ ✳ ☆ ✳ ☆ ✳

The Hermit: For Further Study

Judgment: Deck Reviews

✹ ☆ ✹ ☆ ✹ ☆ ✹ ☆ ✹ ☆ ✹ ☆ ✹ ☆ ✹

About the Authors

Ruth Ann and Wald Amberstone are well-known in the tarot community as highly creative and original teachers. They are founders of the Tarot School and authors of *The Tarot School Correspondence Course* and *Tarot Tips: 78 Practical Techniques to Enhance Your Reading Skills*. They are also the creators of the Readers Studio, an annual national conference for tarot professionals.

Elizabeth Barrette studies tarot and other forms of divination, and collects divinatory tools. She serves as the managing editor of *PanGaia*. She has been involved with the Pagan community for more than eighteen years, and has done much networking with Pagans in her area, including coffeehouse meetings and open sabbats.

Nina Lee Braden, a Scorpio, has had a lifetime fascination with death and dying. However, by using tarot to help her with the grief cycle, she learned more about tarot, about life, about relationships, and about death.

Dallas Jennifer Cobb lives an enchanted life in a waterfront village in Canada. Forever scheming novel ways to pay the bills, she's freed up resources for what she loves most: family, gardens, fitness and fabulous food. When she's not running country roads or wandering the beach, she is writing and daydreaming.

Sally Cragin writes the astrological forecast "Moon Signs" for the *Boston Phoenix* and other newspapers. She is a regular arts reviewer and feature writer for the *Boston Globe*, and edits *Button*, New England's tiniest magazine of poetry, fiction, and gracious living since 1993.

Elizabeth Genco keeps one foot firmly planted in the Northeastern woods and the other in Brooklyn, New York, where she pours her love of myth, magic, old-school horror, and esoterica into comics and other fictions. She and her husband, comics artist Leland Purvis, run a small press called Streetfables. She has been reading tarot and practicing Wicca for over a decade and is an initiate in the Protean and Gardnerian traditions.

✳ ☆ ✳ ☆ ✳ ☆ ✳ ☆ ✳ ☆ ✳ ☆ ✳ ☆ ✳

Mary K. Greer has forty years of tarot experience and, as an author and teacher, emphasizes personal insight and creativity. Mary is a member of numerous tarot organizations and is featured at tarot conferences and symposia around the world. She is the proud recipient of the 2006 Mercury Award from the Mary Redman Foundation in recognition of her ground breaking book *Tarot for Your Self: A Workbook for Personal Transformation*. Her latest book is *Mary K. Greer's 21 Ways to Read a Tarot Card*.

Magenta Griffith has been a Witch for nearly thirty years, and is a founding member of the coven Prodea, which has been celebrating rituals since 1980. She has been a member of the Covenant of the Goddess, the Covenant of Unitarian Universalist Pagans, Church of All Worlds, and several other organizations. She presents workshops and classes at a variety of festivals and gatherings around the Midwest.

Elizabeth Hazel is the author of *Tarot Decoded: Understanding and Using Dignities and Correspondences*, the first primer of tarot dignities. She is an accomplished astrologer and tarotist, and writes a syndicated weekly horoscope column, as well as *newWitch* magazine's "Astro-Spell" column. Liz's articles and artwork have appeared in a variety of tarot, astrology, and earth-religion publications. Her interests include music, art, and alchemical perfumery.

Annie Jones is an aspiring writer, closet artist, and certified yoga instructor. Her work with the cards focuses on providing personal insight and perspective and her goal is to assist people in improving their lives. She is a strong advocate for the mind/body connection and works to help people reconnect with their inner spirit through relaxation and meditation.

Corrine Kenner is the author of *Tall Dark Stranger*, a handbook on using tarot cards for romance; *Tarot Journaling*, a guide to the art of keeping a tarot diary; the *Epicurean Tarot*, the innovative "recipe card" tarot deck published by U.S. Games Systems, Inc.; and *Crystals for Beginners*. She lives in Minneapolis with her husband and three daughters.

Mark McElroy is the author of seven books on tarot; the creator of *The Bright Idea Deck* (Llewellyn), the *Tarot of the Elves* (Lo Scarabeo), and the *Da Vinci Tarot* (Lo Scarabeo); and the editor-in-chief of TheTarotChannel.com.

Leeda Alleyn Pacotti is a naturopathic doctor, specializing in sleep and dream rehabilitation. Her authorship includes texts on natural cures for both professionals and nonprofessionals, although her publishing ventures are wide-ranging and eclectic.

Rachel Pollack is the author of twenty-seven books of fiction and nonfiction, including two award-winning novels and more than a dozen books on tarot. Her books include *The Kabbalah Tree*, *The Forest of Souls*, and *Seeker*, all published by Llewellyn. A visual artist as well as writer, she is the creator of *The Shining Tribe Tarot*, also available from Llewellyn.

Kevin Quigley has been reading and studying tarot for more than ten years. His spiritual practice can be described as being both eclectic and pragmatic. He employs a variety of different perspectives to compare, contrast, conflict, and support each other.

Roslyn Reid teaches yoga and tarot, which she has studied for over twenty-five years. She is currently in training to become a dream-worker. A longtime contributor of art and articles to Llewellyn and other Pagan publications such as *SageWoman* and *Dalriada*, she has also contributed to Susun Weed's book, *Breast Cancer? Breast Health!*

Janina Renée is a scholar of folklore, psychology, medical anthropology, the material culture of magic, ritual studies, history, and literature. She has written five books for Llewellyn: *Tarot Spells*, *Playful Magic*, *Tarot Your Everyday Guide*, *Tarot for a New Generation*, and *By Candlelight: Rites for Celebration, Blessing & Prayer*.

James Ricklef is a Certified Tarot Master—a tarot reader, lecturer, and writer. For many years now, he has been a workshop presenter at the annual Los Angeles Tarot Symposium (LATS). He has also been a featured speaker at the New York Tarot Reader's Studio and at the annual San Francisco Bay Area Tarot Symposium (BATS). He is the author of the award-winning book *Tarot Tells the Tale* and of a book about tarot spreads titled *Tarot—Get the Whole Story*.

Cerridwen Iris Shea longs for a garden. She writes, teaches tarot, cooks, is owned by several cats, and is a fan of ice hockey and thoroughbred racing.

Valerie Sim is a Certified Tarot Grandmaster, and is the listowner of the popular e-mail list "Comparative Tarot." Her first book, *Tarot Outside the Box*, was published in 2004, and she is now at work on her second book, *Shamanic Tarot*. She wrote the "little white book" for the recently published *Comparative Tarot Deck*, and is a former board member and editor for the American Tarot Association. She lives in the foothills of northern California, where she is admittedly a bit of a hermit, pursuing a shamanic path.

Thalassa is the producer of the San Francisco Bay Area Tarot Symposium (SF BATS), founder of Daughters of Divination (DOD), and publisher of *The Belfry*. She teaches and produces divination events in the SF Bay Area, and has presented at the World Tarot Congress, the New York Tarot Festival, PantheaCon, and LATS (LA Tarot Symposium). She lives in San Francisco with a collection of swords, too many books, more tarot decks than one can safely shake a stick at, and a tribe of semi-feral dust bunnies.

James Wells is a Toronto-based tarot consultant, Reiki teacher, workshop facilitator, and writer. Tarot has been a part of his life since 1979 and he's happy to say that tarot is his day-job. His mission is to assist humanity in reaching its full potential, one person at a time. His book, *Tarot for Manifestation*, is a toolbox to help people make their desires a reality. In the rare moments when he's not engaged in tarot-related activities, James enjoys long walks, journaling, reading, time with friends, good food, and well-made martinis.

Gail Wood teaches workshops and classes on alternative spiritualities, Wicca, tarot, ritual, shamanic journeywork, and Reiki. She is the author of *Rituals of the Dark Moon: 13 Lunar Rites for a Magical Path* (Llewellyn, 2001); articles in a variety of pagan publications; and *The Wild God: Meditations and Rituals on the Sacred Masculine* (Spilled Candy, 2006). Her poetry can be found in the 2007 *We'Moon Datebook* and 2007 *We'Moon on the Wall*. She is a member the Coven of the Redtail Hawk, and is high priestess of the Coven of the Heron, both of the RavenMyst Circle.

Winter Wren is a professional tarot reader residing in southeastern Michigan. She became involved with tarot at the age of sixteen and has been reading professionally more than twenty-five years now. She currently serves as Executive President of the American Board for Tarot Certification and is working on completing her own tarot deck. She is assisted in all her projects by Fizzgig, her very large Maine coon cat.

The Fool

Tools for the Journey

Out of the Box

by Thalassa

S o you want to play with a full deck (of tarot cards, that is).
Daunted yet excited, you are eager to hop on the painted
caravan, but probably also mystified by the encrustation of
tradition, hearsay, and lurid depictions of tarot. It certainly makes
a full-throttle approach to tarot slightly more challenging than taking up couture tailoring or philately. Where does one start? More
importantly, what does one do with a pack of tarot cards once it's
in one's eager paws? And *then* what?

These days tarot cards are available everywhere from chain
booksellers and warehouse stores to Ye Olde Spirit Shoppe in the
mall, so it has never been easier to acquire a vast array of decks (one
should be warned from the outset that tarot decks are like potato
chips—it is extremely hard to have just one). Legions of books cry
out from groaning bookstore shelves, promising to enlighten *you*,
the dewy-eyed would-be explorer of the Mysteries. How does one
machete a path through the overgrowth?

It often seems as if the Ideal Scenario is supposed to go a little like this: when the mysterious old woman wrapped in paisley
scarves and bewildering costume jewelry has departed cackling
into the stormy night, leaving you with Your First Deck, you conse-
crate the cards by exposing them to the gibbous moonlight during

a particularly auspicious celestial convergence, followed by wrapping them in virgin Naugahyde and placing them in a hand-hewn rock crystal box which will rest on your Altar of Art. The sacrifice of a goat is optional.

Perhaps you wish there was a handy information sheet similar to this available at your local Card 'n' Candle Shack: "Thank you for purchasing your new *Arcanum 3000 Tarot Deck*! Your deck is designed to provide years of esoteric excitement. Before you start using your *Tarot Deck*, we ask you to first remove it from its box and take a few minutes to acclimate yourself to the plethora of moving parts. The manufacturer would like to point out that by purchasing a *Tarot Deck* you may be exposed to a world of fun, challenge, exploration, and compulsive collecting for which the manufacturer cannot be held responsible. When using your new *Tarot Deck*, be sure to keep all appendages solidly in the physical plane until appropriate astral safety parameters have been established. Warning: playing strip poker with tarot cards may cause you to lose more than your shirt. Having taken proper precautions (enumerated in sub-chapter three of the enclosed Little White Instruction Book [LWB]) you are now free to let the games begin!"

Worry no more, gentle seeker! What follows is your *Triple A-for-Arcanum* guide to a lifetime of metaphysical fun and frolic.

Adopting a Deck

There is a stubborn "tradition" in tarot that insists your first deck must

The Queen of Cups from *Legend: The Arthurian Tarot*

be given to you (see reference to cackling paisley-clad crone above). If you are one of those fortunate souls who have had a deck bestowed upon you, lucky you! Proceed to enjoy the article and try not to rub the noses of the rest of us in your good fortune. On the other hand, not all blessings are bestowed unalloyed. If you were made the recipient of *Crazy Eddie's Cut Rate Cartoon Character Tarot* and it didn't exactly send a shiver through your astral body, despair not. Set it respectfully aside (the back of your sock drawer or in the box with your high school yearbooks should do nicely), then proceed to get yourself something better suited to your needs and taste. You may learn to love it later (or be able to cheerfully gift it to someone else for whom it is a better fit).

Contemplating the acquisition of Your First Tarot Deck is a good time to ask yourself about your primary reason for starting down the primrose path of tarot exploration. Do you wish to read the cards (divination)? Use them primarily as a magical or meditative tool? Decorate your home in an unusually colorful and resonant way? The answers to these questions will help guide you to the deck that is right for the purpose.

Although the guidance of a knowledgeable friend or teacher can be invaluable, your instincts will be the best guide when it comes to finding that just right (for now) deck. In these fortunate times, there is an online wonderland of information and inventory beckoning, and by all means belly up to the cyber-bar to explore the length and breadth of the Tarot Kingdom. However, there is so much that is tactile and visual about tarot that there is great merit in actually handling a deck of potential new friends before plunking down real money. But be assured that whether you spin the magic online shopping wheel or paw through the displays in a "brick and mortar" setting, there is no right or wrong way to decide on a deck.

There are tarotic interpretations of just about every conceivable spiritual tradition, historical epoch, philosophical fashion, or design concept, executed in a giddy range of artistic and conceptual styles. If your taste goes to neo-Platonic existentialist images done in an Aztecish style, I have no doubt that there is a tarot deck certain to tickle your aesthetic somewhere in the wide world. However, some decks do lend themselves more readily than others to beginning study.

If there can be such a thing, the "standard" is the *Rider-Waite-Smith* (known as the *RWS* to aficionados), a deck created early in the last century by the magical artist Pamela Colman "Pixie" Smith under the direction of the English ceremonial magician Arthur Edward Waite. It is one of the most popular, visually accessible, and easily obtained decks, and a staggering number of reinterpretations and variations have been spun from its imagery. An especially valuable feature of *RWS*–type decks is that both the Major and Minor Arcana are completely illustrated, which greatly helps with the "get acquainted" stage.

It is wise to remember, however, that ideology and concepts are all very well, but if the imagery does not speak to you—no matter how breathtaking its metaphysical credentials—it can inhibit your learning (if only by making you resentful that it was forced on you as "The One Deck You Should Be Using To Learn Tarot™"). In this Brave New World of Consumer Choice in metaphysical tools, there is every reason to acquire a deck with which you can happily work, and if the RWS or its variants don't snap your socks, that's completely all right.

Bonus! You do not have stick to your original deck decision. If after the "honeymoon glow" has faded you find that you are not bonding, it's completely acceptable to set the deck aside (perhaps in the front of the sock drawer or with the winter coats) for a later encounter. You may discover its special merits later (or you may simply wish to turn it into metaphysically infused mulch).

Making Friends with Pasteboard
Learning tarot is a non-stop exercise in learning to listen to your inner voice. In the beginning, the best way to make a meaningful connection to the tarot is to form your own direct connection to the cards, and a great beginning exercise is to just look at the darned things. A lot. Try to hear the special voice with which they speak to you. Separate the deck into piles of cards that move you—the ones you especially like, do not especially care for, are disturbed by, etc.—and go through the piles with care and consideration. This will help you develop a baseline impression of what the cards mean to you personally that will later be augmented by your reading and further study. If you like using a journal approach, recording your impressions at this time can be a valuable foundation for future study. These approaches will also serve you admirably whenever you "break in" a new deck.

There are many wonderful and valuable tarot tomes available these days, but they can wait for a little while as you develop your own unique and individual relationship with the cards.

Care & Feeding
Whatever the purpose of your tarot study, remember that, first and foremost, tarot cards are tools. You want them well rested and ready to hand. Many books provide detailed instructions for wrapping, boxing, displaying, and handling your tarot decks. Lots of this information is valuable, but it should be taken as advice rather than Holy Writ.

One of the terrific things about taking up tarot is the accoutrements: the scarves, the bags, the boxes, etc. The only real rule is that if it's beautiful, and if it feels like suitable swathing for your pack of pasteboard darlings, then that is what they should be placed in. Just about anything will do, although this author has a personal animus against Ziploc freezer bags (the cards can't breathe and get cranky).

XI FORTITUDE

Fortitude from *Medieval Enchantment: The Nigel Jackson Tarot*

The same goes with rituals of preparing your cards and putting them to bed: feel free to devise your own protocol. If burning sage makes you giddy, you don't like putting seventy-eight cards under your pillow at night, or you can't remember the Golden Dawn Lesser Banishing Pentagram, just do what makes the experience feel both right *and* special for you.

As fond as many tarotists are of all the trappings—and while such things can be meaningful and delightful—they are not necessary. The primary purpose of all this window dressing is to convey to your innermost self that you are embarking on something wondrous and set apart from the mundane. Whatever creates that misty glow for you is fine with the rest of the unseen realm. By way of example, your author wrapped her first deck in her favorite paisley scarf (not knowing then that said scarf was polyester—*not* a natural fiber) and kept them in a box reeking of cheap sandalwood (it was the '60s after all). We are pleased to report that both cards and student survived just fine.

Other People's Cooties

Endless advice has been offered on the topic of Other People Handling Your Tarot Cards. Frankly, it's completely up to you (beginning to sense a pattern?). Tarot cards are generally beautiful (except those with stinky artwork) and have the added one-two punch of unarticulated archetypal resonance. From their earliest development, the cards have been designed to provoke wonder and a certain mystification. People want to look at them—and often want to touch. You don't have to let them do that if you aren't comfortable, but, as a rule, they (the cards, not the people) aren't going to get cooties or desert you if other people fondle them.

✦ In Conclusion

The tarot gives us magnificent opportunities to access our inner wisdom and to connect to the mysterious universe within and around us. Studying the tarot is an excellent exercise of our abilities to think both critically and creatively. The regular use of the tarot will almost guarantee that you will be engaging in an exciting, challenging, and transformative process of a type which our modern world seldom affords us.

So, gentle seeker of the mysteries: you now have a deck (or decks). You have bonded and you are beginning to get a sense of what to do with it. It has a place to live. You are saddled up and provisioned for a magical ride. Bon voyage! Don't forget to write (and read)!

Twelve Ways to Use Tarot

by Elizabeth Barrette

When most people think about the tarot, the first thing that comes to mind is usually prediction. Yet there is far more to tarot than predicting the (possible) future. Rich in history and mysticism, tarot holds a vast store of symbolism which gives rise to many different applications. Let's take a tour of what you can do with the tarot.

Archetypes

An archetype is an original concept or a broad category that inspires other examples. An archetype recurs throughout literature and culture in many variations, becoming part of the human experience. The tarot relies heavily on archetypes and thus serves as an excellent tool for learning about them. A classic deck works best for this purpose (or else a deck steeped in the archetypes of a specific culture).

The Major Arcana consists entirely of archetypes. These universal figures speak to everyone's experience. To a lesser extent, the Minor Arcana contains some archetypes: the Court Cards represent family members, and the Aces represent the elemental energy of each suit.

Look at the tarot cards in order, and you'll see that they tell a kind of story. The Major Arcana cards illustrate the evolution of a soul from innocence to wisdom, with each archetype representing a step along the way. Suits in the Major Arcana often tell stories of strife (Swords), valor (Wands), romance (Cups), or success (Coins). So the easiest way to study archetypes is to go through the deck in sequence. Each day, pull out the next card and examine its image. Read its interpretation. Compare it to similar motifs. For instance, compare the Emperor to other figures of masculine authority you have encountered. By the end of the deck, you'll be familiar with the most common archetypes.

Counseling

For challenges of a magical or spiritual nature, the tarot can serve as an aid to counseling. Any deck can work for this purpose, as long as you feel comfortable with it; decks with a psychological angle are especially apt. The cards serve as a therapeutic bridge between participants.

Tarot offers at least two approaches here. First, you can use the divinatory aspect of the cards to unearth hidden parts of a problem so they can be dealt with openly. Most introspective and many problem-solving spreads work for this. It's also possible to ask individual questions and draw cards one at a time in response, such as, "What is the best response to this situation?"

Second, you can take a more philosophical approach. Sort through the cards face-up and select one that catches your attention. Consider the card's imagery and interpretive text; search for parallels in your own mind. How do these things relate to your current circumstances? Does anything suggest a possible solution—or complication? You can spin off a single theme into a long exploratory conversation.

Creative Inspiration

Any randomizable set of concepts can provide useful inspiration in times of creative need. Tarot cards work especially well for this purpose because of their vivid imagery and intricate meanings. The Major Arcana cards deal primarily in themes, the Court Cards indicate people, and the pip cards reveal actions and situations. Draw a card and apply it to your needs.

Find a theme for a story, article, poem, or other piece of writing by reading the keywords in a card's interpretation. To choose a setting, examine a card's background and the objects depicted on it. For character inspiration, look for people in a card. Who are they? What are they wearing? How do they relate to each other and to their surroundings? Generate plot twists by following the events or conflicts portrayed in a card. For a touch of whimsy, draw two cards and mix and match the ideas and images they contain.

Don't overlook the visual aspects of a card: cards can suggest decoration schemes for a room, color choices for a quilt, themes for a party—use your imagination.

Daily Meditation

Meditation is the practice of quieting the mind so that you can relax and find tranquility, and it can help to have a focus for your thoughts. Any deck that resonates with you should work with this, but those with an introspective tone or layered meanings are ideal.

Each day, draw one card as a meditative focus. Spend a few minutes looking at it. Imagine yourself stepping into the card. You can talk to people there, pick up objects—do anything that catches your fancy. Afterward, leave the card somewhere you can see it.

Throughout the day, be alert for things that relate to the card's theme. You might encounter objects or situations that remind you of the card. At the end of the day, compare your experiences to the card's interpretation. How much similarity was there?

Dream Interpretation

Dreams rise from the subconscious, intuitive mind toward the conscious, logical mind. Divination takes the reverse route. Therefore, tarot as a means of dream interpretation meets in the middle. For best results, choose a deck with dreamy images, intricate symbolism, or deep personal meaning.

One method for dream interpretation is to sort through the cards face-up, looking at their pictures, to see if something jogs your memory. You may find things in the cards that help you recall more of what you dreamed, and can put the pieces together.

Another method is to customize a reading to answer specific questions about a dream. Shuffle and draw random cards, one per question. For instance, "Why was the armadillo riding a bicycle?" might lead to the Two of Coins, a card about balance.

Finally, your subconscious will happily seize on any handy set of symbols to communicate with your conscious mind. So if you use the tarot frequently, you may find its symbolism appearing directly in your dreams—thus making interpretation easier, as you can look up the card motifs you recognize.

Games

Historical references suggest that tarot began as a card game and later evolved into a divinatory system. Some diviners still use ordinary playing cards for divination, too. Most tarot decks can be used to play relevant games; however, a few modern decks are specially designed for gaming. When possible, use separate decks for play and for divination.

The Italian game *Tarrochi* assigns point values to the cards that don't always correspond to the card's number. Other games use the card's normal face value, and the Fool card has different purposes in different types of games. The Swiss game *Troggu* counts the cards at face value, but the Fool can be used in multiple ways within the same game.

The Aeclectic Tarot website has a "Fun and Games" forum where people play guessing games to figure out which card or deck someone is thinking of, based on different types of clues. Any version of these would make a fun party game, and you can easily invent your own variations.

The Lord of the Rings Tarot Deck and Card Game was carefully designed to allow for divinatory or recreational use. The game evolves into a battle of light against dark, centered around controlling the One Ring—an interesting exercise if you're struggling with gray areas in your life.

Journaling

Journaling overlaps with many other tarot uses. First, of course, you should record the readings you do for later reference. You may also want to write about other explorations you make.

If you make regular entries in a journal and get stuck without an idea, draw a card for inspiration. Write about the card's imagery or interpretation. This also works for recording your daily meditations.

For dream interpretation or card symbolism, draw a card and write down what it means to you—without referencing any outside source.

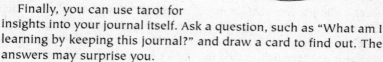

When studying archetypes, elements, or other broad magical motifs, you can use the deck simply to set the theme. Draw a card, identify its theme, and write about the theme instead of the card.

Finally, you can use tarot for insights into your journal itself. Ask a question, such as "What am I learning by keeping this journal?" and draw a card to find out. The answers may surprise you.

Numerology

The tarot system is rich in numeric symbolism. Almost any deck will serve to explore this topic, although some pay more attention to it than others. Avoid the handful of decks that put incorrect numbers of symbols on the pip cards—for instance, having fewer than ten swords on the Ten of Swords. It doesn't matter if the pips are fully illustrated, just numerically correct.

If you compare several decks, you'll notice that the numbering of the Major Arcana varies slightly. Sometimes the Fool is 0, other times I, and more rarely XXII. Justice and Strength may appear as VIII and XI, or vice versa. Which do you prefer?

The number on the card(s) drawn can be interpreted according to your favorite numerology guide. For example, One represents unity and beginning; Two stands for balance or relationships, and so forth. The Major Arcana are read based on their numbers. So are the Minor Arcana cards. The Court Cards are usually numbered after the pip cards, although in some decks they come first. Experiment to see what works for you.

Past Lives

Although many people use tarot to read the future, it works quite well for reading the past. Given the widespread interest in reincarnation, past-life readings are popular. Decks with a historical focus lend themselves especially well to this pursuit.

One approach is to read for clues to when and where a person's previous life took place. This can get complicated, but some spreads are designed for it. If you already have some idea where or when to look, this process can help narrow the focus.

Another common goal is identifying past-life influences on current issues. Skills, habits, affinities, and aversions can all have their roots deep in a previous life. Divining the source makes it easier to deal with those things in the current situation. Again, look for spreads intended for past-life revelation.

Relationship Analysis

This application combines introspective and interactive aspects. It gives a glimpse into two (or more) people and how they relate to each other—and no, it's not just for romance. You can explore parent/child, employer/employee, or other dynamics. However, decks with a romantic flavor are especially suited to couples pursuing this course.

Many spreads exist for reading relationships. It usually pays to design your own, though, based on what you want to learn. The simplest is to choose a number of cards and lay out two rows or columns, one for each of you. Then compare the cards in matching pairs.

Another good spread concept uses an intersecting layout. One set of cards will represent you, another set will represent your partner, and the third will represent your relationship and how the two of you work as a couple. You get much more depth for just a little more complexity.

A more intricate model allows you to build a spread from scratch, asking specific questions about your relationship. You may have questions that apply only to you, only to your partner, to both of you together, or even to other people in your lives. How emotionally compatible are you? What are your reserves of strength? What hidden weaknesses might undermine your relationship? Deep questions can warn you of potential trouble in time to fix it.

In this context, you may approach the cards as divinatory tools revealing the underlying information—or as purely psychological tools that bring issues from your subconscious to your conscious mind. Try interpreting the same reading both ways!

Spellcraft

Wholly outside the realm of divination lies the use of tarot cards as altar tools. The more magically styled decks work best for this, but you can use any that carry a strong charge for you.

A tarot deck is the ultimate in portable witchcraft. Any item needed for a spell can be represented by a picture if you don't have the real thing. Look at the cards and you'll find a vast selection of useful images: mountains, lakes, castles, horses, birds, altars, candles, etc. You can use the four Aces to represent the four main altar tools, or the four elements. The Magician makes a good stand-in for an altar. Invoke deities with a suitable Court Card or one of the Major Arcana.

At home, any card can form the basis of a spell with the same theme. For romance, choose the Lovers or the Two of Cups; for success, the Sun; for wealth, the Ten of Pentacles; and so forth. Use the imagery in the card to inspire your altar setup in terms of colors and other props.

Some spells concern the tarot itself. For example, if you get a very positive reading, you might cast a spell to pour energy into manifesting that result. Use the significator or outcome card as a focus. Conversely, if a really troublesome card comes up in a reading, you can work magic to change its position or replace it with a different card, thus putting energy into altering the course of events. Always remember that divination shows possibilities, not guarantees: if you don't like where you're headed, change your actions and that will usually change your path.

Symbolism

In much the same way as archetypes, other kinds of symbolism can be learned using the tarot. Choose a deck that runs to complex pictures and fully illustrated pip cards, so that you have plenty of images to work with. The most thorough way to study tarot symbolism is to go through the whole deck one card at a time, although you can also draw random cards for study if you wish.

The card name, its number, and its whole picture have a broad meaning that relates to the card's theme. These are customarily covered in the interpretive text for the deck. Beyond that, every object, person, or piece of landscape in the picture also has a meaning—which may or may not appear in the text. Some interpretations are quite famous, such as the Hermit's lamp, which represents enlightenment and guidance. For more obscure motifs, you may need to look up their meanings in a dictionary of symbols.

Repeating this exercise with different decks gives you an optimum way to learn the symbolism of other cultures.

These are just some of the many things you can do with tarot.

Some of these activities also apply to other types of divinatory tools besides the tarot; for instance, you can do daily meditations with ogham or use runes for creative inspiration. Experiment to find new approaches. The more you work with your magical equipment, the better you will know it and the better it will serve you.

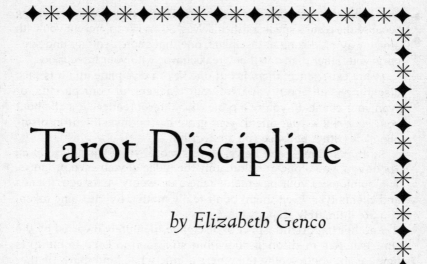

Tarot Discipline

by Elizabeth Genco

Okay, let's have a show of hands of the folks who were browsing the table of contents. How many of you read the title of this article and dropped everything to flip to this page?

Not a single one, eh? I'd like to say that I'm surprised, but in truth, that's exactly what I expected. Let me guess: the word "discipline" didn't exactly start a fire in your belly. It's okay, you can tell me. It doesn't fill me up with zeal and glee, either. But I've made my peace with it, and I'm the better tarotist for it. Here's how, and why.

The word "discipline" lives next door to the voices in my head that constantly kvetch that I'm doing *this* wrong or *that* wrong and *"why are we bothering, again?"* I really don't need more of those, thank you very much. Until recently, discipline has always felt like one of those nebulous boundary lines drawn in the sand by others (read: authority figures; boo, hiss), always moving just out of my reach like a carrot on a stick. Also, like many people, I learned early that the word "discipline" is synonymous with "no fun whatsoever." Discipline's big point in life seems to be to remind me of my failings. So why explore it, let alone shoot for it?

Because it is good for you. It can take a practice—tarot, in this case—further than you'd ever get without it. It's no secret that you'll get more out of those things that you put yourself into; discipline is a way of throwing yourself into good work. Discipline is worth cultivating because the results speak for themselves. So I'd like to present you with a new way of looking at discipline, one that shores you up and supports you rather than one that wreaks havoc with your insecurities.

In my experience, there is but one key to discipline and it is this: discipline is all about you. Not your teachers, or your parents, or even your clients (if you're a professional tarot reader). It's all about you: *your* skills, *your* talent, *your* growth. The investment in discipline is worth it because *you* are worth it.

So that's some good news. Here's more: since discipline is all about you, you alone are ultimately the judge of your own progress. The opinions of your parents, teachers of twenty years ago, friends and clients (yes, even them) don't really matter. By the same token, you are ultimately responsible, too.

Another important aspect of discipline (definitely dwarfed by the One True Key mentioned above but still good to keep in mind) is time. As in, you're going to be here a little while, and that's neither good nor bad but *just is*, so, onward. Discipline works its magic over time and in small doses; repetition is the key to skill-building and growth. Repetition works over time. To be disciplined merely means that you are spending time on a pursuit in a systematic way—one that is designed by you and therefore completely within your control (and, therefore, need not be unpleasant or scary). Time and discipline work together to bring results.

Once you realize that discipline is really all about you and that time is on your side, it becomes a tool rather than a terror. Nonetheless, it can be difficult to wrap one's head around the idea of discipline as

"good" instead of equivalent to "hot pokers in the eyeballs." Here are a few strategies that have helped me to shift my thinking.

Drop the baggage. When it comes to discipline, a lot of us have bad memories of overbearing teachers or parents. Maybe they were well-intentioned, but all you're left with is a head full of old voices and self-doubt, neither of which will serve you very well. Letting them go can be one of the biggest challenges you face. To begin, identify them, one by one. Figure out who's hanging around in your brain and tripping you up. Thank them for their time, but it's about *you*, thank you very much. Tell them that you have work to do, then get back to business. Lather, rinse, repeat as often as needed.

This can feel a little silly and awkward at first, but it really does work. If you keep doing it, those voices eventually take the hint. Remember the secret ingredients of time and repetition.

Choose new archetypes. Is the Emperor the king of discipline in your mind, with his big stick, hard eyes, and perpetual frown? You can give that the boot too, if that's not working for you. Maybe you respond better to the nurturing of the Empress. As I've mentioned, discipline is ultimately all about you. It's a way to take care of yourself, something that the Empress knows a thing or two about. Or, discipline can bring you mastery and control over a subject, so you can let the Chariot be your guide. Look to the Hermit for reminders of the wisdom that comes from patience, time, and self-questioning. Strength knows that the lion inside responds much better to a compassionate touch. You are not limited to one view of discipline; you get to pick what works for you (more about that in a minute).

Keep the end in mind. So what's the point of all the work? Where do you want to be? What do you want to accomplish? Remember, these are your goals, not someone else's goals. The only requirement is that they're compelling enough *to you* to warrant all the effort that you put in. Formulate some goals—I mean the big, juicy kind that move mountains—and write them down in your tarot notebook. Think of them often, especially when you're working on the stuff that doesn't exactly send you running for the cards. You're not doing the work because someone else says that you have to. You're doing the work for your own reasons.

Make the process as enjoyable as possible. Why shouldn't you? This isn't calculus class (though I would argue that you should make that as enjoyable as possible, too). This is one of those ostensibly obvious points that can get lost in the shuffle. It's true that not everything you do to reach your goals will be fun, but that doesn't mean that you shouldn't try to have as much fun as possible.

Let's say that you hate memorization, arguably one of those things you'll face at least a little of during your tarot studies. Perhaps index cards summon intense, viscerally unpleasant memories of seventh-grade spelling tests. What can you do to make memorization less of a drag? Maybe you can invite a friend over and have him read the card meanings aloud from your chosen book (or design your own from books and your own experience), then recite what he said back to you, complete with dramatic flourishes. Or pick a couple of cards, go over the meanings together, and then put the knowledge to use by performing mock readings for one another. Take breaks often for drinks and gossip. Make it a regular thing.

Discipline does require being objective, and yes, that may mean spending some time on things that you don't like. But you don't have to work with the tools provided by a writer or a teacher if they make you break out in hives. If you don't like index cards, then don't use index cards. There is always more than one way to tackle a problem—find the one that works best for you. Remember, discipline is all about you.

Enlist a buddy. Speaking of inviting friends over, you don't have to limit their involvement to the things that you don't like. Partnership in goal-setting and skill-building has a long history (it's classic dieting advice), and with good reason. A partner can keep you going when you're ready to give up, or merely give you a nudge when you're flagging. Partners can also hold each other accountable and remind each other of what's important: your goals. They can also help you troubleshoot when things aren't going well, and give you feedback.

Schedule time with yourself. It might be strange to think of it as such, but time is one of those great equalizers among individuals. Maybe there will never be "enough time," but we all get exactly the same amount in a day. Being judicious with your time is one of the fundamentals of self-care. Your needs and goals are just as important as those of your job, your kids, the chores, and your significant other, so take what's rightfully yours by scheduling some iron-clad time for tarot on the calendar. Put it in pen, not in pencil. If you associate schedules with rigidity, remember that you're setting the schedule and that time can be whenever you take it. And it's time for *you*, not a schedule of must-do's. As you may have heard, discipline is all about you.

Question the process constantly. Applying yourself to any new pursuit is itself a learning process; the way you get the most out of learning is by constantly asking questions. We're talking about your goals and dreams here, so why run on autopilot? When you have missed a couple of classes or scheduled dates with yourself, take a minute to sit down and ask yourself *why*. The question is for the purpose of self-examination, not judgment: don't beat yourself up.

Take a look at those activities you're avoiding—the stuff you think you "should" do but don't want to do. Why don't you like them? What's keeping you from tackling them head-on? Write the answers down. By identifying what's really bugging you and writing it down, you put it in perspective. Usually (not always, but usually) the problem is bigger in your head than it is in reality. Even when it isn't, you can get objective about the problems when you identify them. You can move it from the emotional realm of Cups to the intellectual realm of Swords, where you can find solutions.

While you're questioning what's bugging you, also ask yourself, "Is this something that I *really* need to do?" Do you think you need to do it because "that's the way it's always done" or because "so-and-so amazing author" says so? Is it relevant to your goals? If your goal is to become a professional tarot reader, learning how rich esoteric disciplines such as Kabbalah and alchemy have been applied to tarot can definitely help you. But is it required? You'd need to answer that for yourself based on your own goals, but the answer might very well be no.

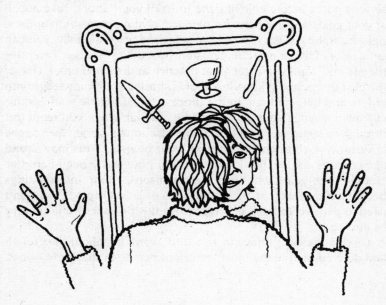

Your time is precious, so it behooves you to constantly evaluate how you spend it. When you make the most of your time, you show yourself the greatest respect. Making the most of your time means ditching the things you don't need, including guilt.

Resistance is also a good opportunity for a goals check. Are your goals relevant and current? If it's getting harder and harder to put in the time, maybe you've outgrown your goals or have moved in a new direction. Identifying your new goals will help get you back on track.

Everything in moderation. Being disciplined doesn't mean asking yourself for more than you're able to give. It means making small, regular steps toward the goals of your own design. You'll get a lot more out of fifteen well-spent, carefully chosen minutes than two hours on an activity you hate. Small chunks of time are fine—and they add up. Take breaks often.

Give yourself rewards. As the saying goes, you'll catch more flies with honey than vinegar. New decks are a great reward and can feed right back into the process when you incorporate them into your work. If buying decks isn't your thing, then how about a class or a new book? You can give yourself completely unrelated rewards too, of course. If you're working with a friend, you can reward each other with small gifts. Words of encouragement also work wonders and are another great reason to find a buddy.

Reap the benefits. You don't have to put yourself through the serious paces before enjoying the fruits of your labors. Take a look at your goals and see how you can actively take ownership of them right from the get-go. If your goal is to read professionally, you can get a taste of that almost immediately by reading for open, receptive friends now (and you'll get great practice at the same time). One of the best things about knowing tarot is sharing your knowledge with others and helping them in the process. Most people you read for will acknowledge your efforts and be grateful; when you really get through to someone, it's like nothing else in the world. Turn to the tarot to work through situations in your own life. This may sound like obvious advice, but I can't tell you how many beginners I've met over the years who won't let themselves jump into readings because they feel that they "don't know enough yet." You don't need to deprive yourself of the good stuff—it's yours from the very beginning.

Discipline doesn't have to be a dirty word. It's about the growth and development of the most important person in the world—you!

Shamanic Tarot

by Gail Wood

Everyone who studies, loves, and works with the tarot approaches the cards from a wealth of perspectives: spiritual, intellectual, philosophical, and more. These viewpoints add to the study of tarot and enrich the wisdom teachings of the cards. From rigorous scholarly historical study to open-ended intuitive approaches, all those who work with the cards create new pathways for debate, understanding, and knowledge of the tarot. This in-depth interaction has taken place over several centuries so that the lore of tarot is deep, rich, and diverse.

There are those who walk between the worlds; to the sound of the drum beating the rhythm of the heart, they move into trance. In trance, the seeker's soul moves into the worlds of spirit, seeking the power of knowledge to heal, succeed, and thrive. These walkers do this work for themselves and for their community. Their work is called shamanism, a practice which also has a rich tradition of wisdom, lore, and knowledge.

Shamanic practice is a set of skills and techniques wherein the practitioner voluntarily moves into altered states of consciousness, seeking information and power to aid self and the community. These altered trance states move the awareness of the practitioner to interact and communicate with beings in other realms of existence. These walkers between the worlds, as shamans are often called, travel into hidden realities in our physical world and to worlds unseen, generally referred to as the Upper World and the Lower World. Connecting all the worlds is the World Tree, *Axis Mundi*, which allows us to travel between the worlds and through the hidden mysteries of our own physical reality, referred to as the Middle World. This is an ancient technique found throughout the world and is in use today.

The term "shaman" comes from the language of the Tungus people of Siberia and means "one who is excited, moved, and raised." This excitement refers to the trance state of the shaman as well as the tool-kit of skills used by the shaman; skills that include lucid trance work, singing, storytelling, and dancing. It is the trance state that distinguishes shamanic practices from other meditative and healing practices. This altered state of deliberate and aware trance is achieved to the rhythm of the beating drum or a rattle. It is an ecstatic state in which the shaman moves outside of the self into hidden and unseen realms of spirit, the Upper and Lower World, and through the hidden magic of the Middle World. As they journey, shamans are aided by spirit helpers: guides that manifest in many forms and include animals, deities, and humans. Typically, an animal spirit guide is called a power animal and is a significant tranformative guide for the shaman; a deity or human guide is considered a powerful spiritual wisdom teacher. Most shamanic practitioners have a number of guides and teachers to aid them.

Shamanic practice entered the industrial world through the work of anthropologist Michael Harner, whose book *The Way of the Shaman* (HarperSanFrancisco, 1990) introduced what he called "core shamanism" to the public. Through his Foundation for Shamanic Studies, many people throughout the world have been taught shamanic techniques for self-awareness, healing, and service to their community.

These techniques and skills can be used in the study of tarot because the images and symbolism of the pictures speak directly to our own ecstatic selves. In turn, our own sense of the mysterious reaches out and touches our connection to the other worlds. It is my belief that the cumulative magical, psychic, intellectual, and emotional energy invested in the cards over the centuries has created similar energetic worlds in all the other realities.

Frequently, cards and characters from the cards have shown up in my shamanic journeywork. When I turned fifty years old, I did a series of shamanic journeys to the Ancient Ones of the elements. In each journey I met a deity who handed me a tarot card. This signaled to me that I needed to merge my shamanic practice with my study and use of tarot. A year or so ago, I was seeking guidance on a question I can no longer remember. The drumbeat began its steady beat of 200 to 225 beats per minute; I sank into a deep trance. Later, I wrote this in my journal:

> I began at my usual journey-place, a large maple tree where I was met by my animal spirit guide, a polar bear. I climbed onto his back and he flew upwards to the Upper World where I was met by my spirit teacher, this time in the form of a middle-aged woman. She walked with me and then suddenly transformed into a woman I recognized as the Empress from the *Rider-Waite-Smith* tarot. She took me to a set of French doors, obviously a gateway to another huge world of vision and sensation. She opened the doors and told me to stand on the threshold and look. Not just look, she said, but truly see. As I focused my vision, I saw forests of Swords, Fools dancing along cliffs, and ocean waves offering up golden Cups to the shore. My teacher then said, Not only can you consult the cards; you can also journey to this world for inspiration and knowledge. You will be able to experience this world as you journey deep inside. Then she went behind me and pushed me over the threshold.

Being pushed over a threshold is an initiatory practice in many kinds of religious and spiritual traditions, a beginning point for students to find greater awareness and wisdom. This was my call to approach tarot from a shamanic perspective.

Seeking a Guide

It occurred to me at some point, as I began to merge my shamanic meditation practice with my study of tarot, that I needed a guide for the process. Traditionally, shamanic practitioners seek guides from the other worlds to aid them in specific tasks or issues. Already well into the process, I was still struggling with how the two practices worked together. It was a far from seamless process until I found a guide. According to my usual practice when I went into a trance meditation, I stated my intention to find a guide. I began my journey in a canoe on a river that met another river. I paddled into the merging rivers where the water became turbulent and I began to get very wet. I looked up and saw a huge raven flying in front of me. As I followed the raven in my canoe, the journey became easier. At some point, the raven flew to the bow of the canoe, and I was able to ask if it was my guide. The raven made clear that I was asking an obvious question, and then replied, "Yes." The call-back drumbeat sounded and I returned to my living space, inspired to a deeper exploration of shamanism and tarot.

Seeking a guide is an excellent beginning journey for the tarot reader–turned–shamanic practitioner. The shamanic process can be truly transformational, bringing new knowledge and wisdom to the seeker. The work a shamanic practitioner does with the tarot not only enhances her own knowledge but adds to the culminated wisdom found in all the realms. If you have never done any shamanic work, some preliminary work is advisable so that you feel comfortable with the method. A good solid introductory work, accompanied by a drumming CD, is Sandra Ingerman's *Shamanic Journeying: A Beginner's Guide* (Sounds True, 2004). Many practitioners will caution you about the dangers of traveling into the worlds of the shaman. If you practice and treat the process with respect by learning the skills well, you will be able to journey safely. After all, living in this physical world requires that we take the proper measures against danger and risk without becoming paralyzed by the fear of threat.

When you are comfortable with the process, go on the journey to seek your tarot teacher-guide. Within the journey, go to a place in nature that is familiar to you and state an intention similar to "I am going to seek a tarot teaching guide." Breathe deeply and go into a trance, either by using one of the shamanic tapes or CDs

available or by drumming for yourself. Be sure to keep a journal of your trance work.

Shamanic Journeying

When I teach shamanic techniques, I often use guided visualizations to help students overcome their often unacknowledged resistance to trance work. A success in visualization leads them to expect success in journeywork. One common meditation is to ask the students to choose a tarot card, and then guide the group through a meditative visualization into the world of the card. The visualization asks them to look at the card until they can "see" the card when they close their eyes. As they begin to meditate, I ask them to see the card grow life-sized. Then they put their hands on the frame of the card and step over the threshold. I guide them further into the world of the card, asking them to notice smells, sights, and sounds. After a short time, I leave them to explore the world of the card on their own. Then I guide them back the way they came, ask them to step out of the card, and shrink the card back to its usual size. Then they open their eyes. This meditation can be adapted for your shamanic journey work and is very useful in getting to know the cards, and internalizing and personalizing your understanding of them. The difference between guided visualization and shamanic trance is the immediacy and intensity of the experience.

The tarot journey can begin with a small amount of preparation, just as you would with any intense study or meditation. I tell my students that when they begin a shamanic journey to state their intention three times as they start their work. So take the card and gaze at it, noting those things that catch your attention. Then prepare for the journey. As the drumbeat begins, state your intention three times: "I am going to travel into the world of the [name] card, seeking insight." Allow your journey to unfold. The drumming should last around twenty minutes, and when you return, take some time to write down the wisdom of your journey. You will find that there are many new insights to be gained from regularly journeying into selected cards of different decks.

Standing in the Body of the Tarot

Another very exciting process is trance postures, a practice I refer to as "standing in the body of the cards." Trance postures are based on the work of anthropologist Felicitas Goodman in works such as *Where the Spirit Rides the Wind: Trance Journeys and Other Ecstatic*

Experiences (Indiana University Press, 1990). She theorized that many of the small statues found in indigenous and shamanic cultures were actually the stance that shamans took when they walked between the worlds. In my practice, this has proven to be an effective way to not only find the wisdom of the cards but to actually "get into the head" of a particular figure in the cards. For example, standing in the stance of the *Rider-Waite-Smith* magician, with one hand raised to the sky and the other hand pointing to the earth, I got a deeper understanding of who the Magician is and how he relates to the world he inhabits.

One April Fools' Day, I co-taught a class, and we used this technique. We had a variety of Fool cards from more than two dozen decks available for students to choose. They chose a card and then stood in the posture of the Fool in the chosen card. Their postures ranged from the almost skipping Fool in the traditional *Rider-Waite-Smith* to the *Animals Divine Tarot*, where the Fool is represented by coyote. The two students who chose the animal-based deck got on their hands and knees and emulated the stance of the coyote found on the card. Tarot students with little or no shamanic experience were able to move into meditative space and follow the wisdom of the Fool card. Students found that the information they received ranged from validation of their spiritual path or additional knowledge about a particular issue to an insight that helped someone remember the meaning of the Fool card.

The real key to seeking and gaining wisdom through shamanic journeywork is not to use new and exciting techniques each time, but to continue consistently practicing the art. Practice is important to the process of learning the knowledge and magic of tarot. It takes intention and attention. While the framework for trance and study in both practices may remain the same, the insights and variations of vision are infinite, beautiful, and wonderful. In a merged world, interaction with the tarot joins shamanism as an exploration of the ecstatic, and the lore and knowledge of both traditions becomes layered with new textures, new magic, and new mysteries. Through study and trance, new, deep, powerful wisdom becomes available to all seekers.

Motley Thoughts

by *Thalassa*

E nvision, if you will, the Major Arcana as one of those amusement park boat rides that glide through moist and faintly electric darkness interspersed with jolts of light and action. As you float gently down this endless hall, each Trump appears as a vividly illuminated, multi-dimensional, mixed-media diorama filled with images and associations stretching from ancient archetypes and musty clichés to curiously dynamic resonances and the specters of modern zeitgeist. Float by the Emperor—gravely clad in a suit of armor (which morphs into an Armani suit)—oozing gravitas as the very exemplar of power, authority, and ossified digestion. Drift languidly past the Star—shimmering in cosmic plasma, diffused astral light, iridescent rhinestones, and maidenly grace. Cover your ears as Gabriel blows his horn, and dodge the ribbon candy as the World androgyne dances in triumph (colliding with Shiva as he performs his rumba of unmaking, but that's another turn of the Wheel).

At the beginning of a branch in the stream—no, toward the end (*oops*) just around the corner (*wait a minute*) slightly beyond the comfortable line of sight—appears the Fool and his accoutrements: warbling eldritch melodies heedlessly off-key, dancing around his dog, thumbing his nose at passersby, tottering on the precipice of ordinary experience, occasionally mooning the audience. Fascinated, one hesitates to draw too close, but the current will eventually take you there anyway.

The Fool is the Key to Everything and Nothing. Put on your bells and boogie to the edge.

By examining the variegated realm of the mad outcast we can learn a great deal about the tarot, the universe, and ourselves. The sacred and secular traditions of every culture spin extrapolations on the light and shadow—the danger and attraction—of the Madman, the Clown, the Outlaw, the Jester. In other words, the Fool.

In the Renaissance card game from whence the tarot derives, the Fool had a deliberately ambiguous role. His appearance in the game initiated a sort of field experiment in controlled chaos management. His depictions ranged from masterless vagabond in the hedgerow to wild man on the blasted heath to madcap, bell-spangled jester. By the time the game and the deck were more or less standardized, he had been given the number that is no number—zero (the great mathematical show-off).

In the late eighteenth century, as the tarot began to acquire more occult connotations, the Fool was often designated the Alpha—or at other times assigned to be the Omega—of the tarot pack. However, he could show up just about anywhere: there was no telling where some savant would position Trump 0. As his position in the arcade of the Arcana shifted, he began to sport a wider range of tattered finery and acquire sundry esoteric functions, not to mention a diverse assortment of animal companions.

As the tarot continued to develop over time, the Fool acquired a mythic luster to his antic arcane duties. Waite called him "a prince from another world on his travels through this one," and Pixie Smith clothed him like a Renaissance lordling on holiday. Crowley connected him with Dionysius, among other wild gods ("O Fool! begetter of both I and Naught, resolve this Naughty Knot!" Uncle Al—no stranger to madness and trickery—chortles in the *Book of Lies*) and Lady Harris surrounded him with an overwhelming entourage of colorful props, symbolic stage dressing, and lively animal associates.

At some point, a charming tradition developed among tarotists that the Fool carries all he needs in his pack. Obviously

The Fool from *The Gilded Tarot*

THE FOOL

not the sort of archetype to be toting a toothbrush and a change of underwear, his knapsack is rumored to contain little but a deck of tarot cards (although one wonders whether there's also a Zagat guide for the Upper Astral Hilton chain, but that's the stuff of another essay).

A more mystical view of the Trump That Is No Trump identifies him with Parsifal, part of a long line of Holy Fools and Divine Clowns. The childlike simplicity of his madness invests him with a purity that provides a sort of all-access backstage pass to the workings of the universe.

That's a lot of motley for a Fool's shoulders to bear.

From time immemorial, in life as well as archetype, the Fool has been set apart. The Fool has had his social filters ripped away and can no longer be expected to participate in "normal" existence. Thus stripped of pretence and ordinary social obligations, he often sees through artifice, casts away obligation, severs contact with mundane reality. Doing what we will not do, saying what we dare not say, living where we cannot live, he is uncomfortable and inconvenient. As he roams the world bereft of the protective cocoon of consensus reality, the Fool is prey to more than the demons in his head. His concerns swing from comically limited in scope one moment to eerily penetrating the next. Like clouds across a windy sky (and just about as predictable) his emotions race across his interior landscape and escape into the everyday world with a shiver of dissonance. Wackyness may ensue, or something quite different. It is therefore no surprise to see him capering in the theatre, shambling in the streets, and shimmering ambivalently through the tarot. He is chorus and obstacle, maker of trouble and of matches. He raises hackles, contends with elementals, turns balloons into poodles. By observing his range of derangement, we examine what happens when the veil is rent and the cultural controls are skewed, whether as a caper across a stage, a shamble toward skid row, or a tarot card flying irrationally from a pack.

Since ancient times the jester could speak truth to power in a way that ordinary folk dared not (and the great tradition of the Jester lives even now—think Mort Sahl and Robin Williams). The works of Shakespeare are teeming with Fools and Clowns who help push the story to its appropriate conclusion by way of a bramble patch of hilarious antics and provocation. Costard, Feste, Hamlet's Gravedigger—a great gibbering, flaunting, fleering panoply of zanies—pull the wool from unwilling eyes and help propel a story through blockades of social convention and narrative constipation. The Fool in *As You Like It* is named aptly named Touchstone.

A touchstone tests the mettle of a substance by drawing forth its essence. In other words, it defeats trickery through a form of artifice. Similarly, we react to madness and foolery according to our temperament: we sputter and get offended, we gather the folds of our costume and flee, we laugh and play along. And yet, not all Fools are funny. The poor nameless fellow who keeps Lear company on the heath is cursed both by seeing too clearly and by being unable to do anything besides offer cold comfort. In the end, it is good to be occasionally reminded that we all have our inner madwoman in the attic, albeit under varying degrees of lock and key. The Fool draws our attention to that internal Mardi Gras. What we do with the revelation is not his affair.

Clowns and Fools were almost interchangeable until modern times: often clever, just as often annoying, generally beyond the pale, but useful to move the plot along (or keep the king on his toes). In today's world, Clowns are set apart. Their breed of wackyness is more contrived, owing more to the trickster gods who shoot well-aimed raspberries at human fumbling and hubris (Coyote, Loki, et al) than to Bedlam. Their exaggerated makeup and raucous actions fascinate, entertain, but also disturb the status quo, maddening yet somehow necessary. In this they share the same outcast radiance—that sense of inconvenient truth—the Fool has always trailed in his wake.

So ancient, ambivalently charged an archetype is too often dodged, glossed over, made safe. From this moment, dear reader, resolve not to look at the Fool, wherever you may find him, in the old complacent way. Trump 0 affords us an opportunity to examine these difficult issues, far beyond our comfort zone, in a way that is both safe and dynamic. Sometimes it is wisdom to play the fool. Sometimes we have no choice but to make the foolish choice, and there is no way out but through the rabbit hole. There are times we need to trust that there is a safety net just outside the frame of the picture. Folly even occasionally leads to wisdom.

The Fool capers between these realms in manic glee and sometimes begs (sometimes drags) us to cartwheel along with him. He reminds us to not be afraid to occasionally tilt reality on its ear, shake the bottle (and your booty), rattle the bells, and stir up your life!

> Full of high sentence, but a bit obtuse
> At times, indeed, almost ridiculous—
> Almost, at times, the Fool.
> —T.S. Eliot

Introductions at Court

by James Ricklef

In my beginning tarot classes, I have observed that students often find the Court Cards to be the hardest to understand. Perhaps the personality issues that these cards raise are more difficult to grasp than the everyday circumstances and events of the numbered cards (Ace through Ten) or the spiritual archetypes of the Major Arcana.

In this article, we will explore techniques designed to help you understand the basics of and assign meaning to the Court Cards, which you can then apply to any particular deck. And because these fundamental meanings will arise from your own reasoning and intuition, they are simple to learn and easy to remember.

We'll begin with a brief look at the characteristics of the four tarot suits, followed by an examination of the Court Card ranks. However, before embarking on this discussion, it is important to mention a couple of points about the naming and classification systems that we will be using here in order to establish a common basis for our discussion.

First of all, I generally use a set of elemental associations for the tarot suits that is common, although not universal. (If you happen to use a different scheme, please bear with me, as the purpose of this article is to demonstrate techniques, not to enforce specific dogmas.) Also, when discussing the Court Cards it is important to clarify the issue of gender. Sometimes the gender of a Court Card implies the gender of a person it signifies, but generally each of these cards can indicate or comment upon either a male or female. However, so that I won't have to continually use cumbersome phrases like "he or she," I will refer to the Pages and Queens as "she" and the Knights and Kings as "he."

Let's start now by taking a brief look at some characteristics of the four tarot suits, which will provide a foundation upon which to build our understanding of the Court Cards in those suits.

The suit of Wands (with an elemental association of fire) is the suit of energy and is concerned with enthusiasm and passion, spirit and confidence, and adventure and risk taking. The Cup cards (associated with water) deal with the mysteries of the heart as they focus on our emotions, such as love, compassion, and satisfaction on the one hand and ennui, discontent, and grief on the other. They are also concerned with our relationships, from romance to family life to friendships. The suit of Swords (associated with air) is concerned with our intellect, ideas, and decisions. It also rules over the domain of communications, and thus covers conflicts and disagreements as well. The Pentacles (associated with earth) deal with health and well being, work and money, and practicality and stability. They are concerned with things that are concrete and grounded in the material world, and as a result they also deal with our sense of security, worth, and value.

The Queen of Pentacles from *The Gilded Tarot*

QUEEN OF PENTACLES

Now let's see how we might understand the Court Cards by combining interpretations of their ranks with the characteristics of the four suits noted above. We will begin with a look at how the Court Card rankings may be related to hierarchical or organizational levels.

We can think of the Pages as people who are subservient to us or who are lower in the pecking order of an organization. So, for example, the Page of Pentacles might indicate someone who works for us or someone whose position at work is considered lower than ours. On the other hand, it can say that we should prepare to do some sort of work that we consider to be beneath us.

The Knights may be seen as our peers or equals in a hierarchy, such as classmates, colleagues, or business associates. As an example, we might find that the Knight of Swords advises us to lend credence to the opinions of a co-worker, or it might suggest that we should communicate better with such a person.

Finally, we may see the Queens and Kings as people who outrank us in some way, with the Queens being those who are supportive, sympathetic, or responsive to our needs, while the Kings are more controlling, authoritative, or domineering. We also may consider the Queens as representing those who govern by consensus or persuasion as opposed to the Kings, who rule by force or fiat. Thus, we might interpret the Queen of Cups as indicating someone who can give us helpful advice for our love lives, while the King of Cups may recommend that we assume a more assertive role in a relationship.

Another way of looking at the Court Cards is to see them in terms of a learning curve, or as milestones on our road to maturity. In that case, we can think of the Pages as portraying a phase in which we are learning something new or as offering advice on how to begin a new chapter in our lives. For example, the Page of Swords might say that the relentless curiosity of a child is what we need in order to solve a problem, or it can signify someone in our life who has that characteristic.

Coming next on this path, the Knights indicate a stage wherein we are actively exploring something that we have recently learned. Perhaps we are testing our new knowledge or skills through trial and error, or maybe now that we have learned a bit about something, we think that we know it all, like a stereotypical teenager. An application of this concept could be to see the Knight of Wands as someone who is impatient or impulsive, as someone who wants to act right now rather than "waste" time planning. Alternatively, this card may tell us that our courage or resolve is being tested.

Then there are the Queens and Kings, both of which have achieved a superior level of mastery and maturity, although in very different ways. The Queens, with their "feminine" qualities of creativity and nurturing, point toward expanding our knowledge or finding creative ways to exercise skills that we have mastered. The "masculine" Kings, on the other hand, indicate self-confident experts in the aspect of life indicated by their suits, and they tend to be more dictatorial than the

Queens, who typically encourage and support others. Also, the self-assurance displayed by the Kings is born of competence and experience, which is in contrast to the Knights, whose confidence is often reckless, hasty, or presumptuous.

So, for example, the creativity and nurturing of the Queens may reveal itself in the Queen of Pentacles as the advice to be practical, resourceful, or generous, while the domineering nature of the Kings might lead us to see the King of Pentacles as someone who maintains strict control of his financial affairs. For an extreme illustration of the difference between these two cards, compare Ebenezer Scrooge to Mr. Fezziwig (young Scrooge's boss in the warehouse where he apprenticed) in Dickens's *A Christmas Carol*.

Finally, there is a fundamental truth about the Court Cards that should guide our use of them in the course of our tarot readings. This is the fact that everyone contains some element of each and every one of the Court Cards. In other words, our personalities may be thought of as tapestries woven of threads from sixteen skeins, one for each Court Card. One particular thread may be more prevalent than the others, or one may dominate in some specific area or time of our lives, but although no one is completely a Page of Pentacles (for example), any Court Card may signify a specific person by his or her most predominant traits. Quite often, though, the Court Cards focus attention on that part of our own personality that is most germane to the message of the reading, such as a character flaw that is blocking our personal development, a trait that we need to acquire, or a quality that we should accentuate.

Of course, there are countless ways to interpret these cards, and as your tarot journey progresses, you will find those that suit you the best. However, what I have described here is an intuitive technique that helps tarot students become more comfortable with reading the Court Cards.

So now it's time to do a bit of exploring on your own. If you are having difficulties understanding the Court Cards, try the method outlined above. Think about what each of the Court Card ranks generally suggests to you, and then apply those meanings to the significance of the four tarot suits.

This is a great way to launch or accelerate your voyage of discovery with these sixteen cards, but it is only the beginning. Once you have laid this foundation for your understanding of the Court Cards, experience will continue to improve your tarot skills and deepen your ability to recognize and make sense of the individual voices of the Court Cards in any tarot reading you do.

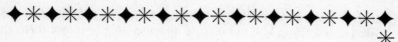

Tarot Vocab

by Elizabeth Genco

When I was eighteen, I spent two and a half months backpacking through Europe with two friends. Out of the ten (or so) countries we visited, France was my favorite. Thanks to four years of intense classes, I was a decent French speaker; in fact, I was even mistaken for French a couple of times. We spent a week in Paris, where I navigated the streets easily and held impromptu conversations with the locals.

After we moved on to the next stops, it became clear just how much my ability to communicate contributed to my positive experience in France (aside from the fact that, you know, we were in *Paris*). In Spain, Italy, and Germany (the most difficult of them all), I was as lost as the next "clueless American" tourist. I knew a bit of Spanish, mostly gleaned from fifth-period language-class crossovers in high school; Italian is similar enough to French and Spanish that I could tease meanings out of things like street signs with the help of a dictionary and a few minutes to spare. But for the most part, I was at the mercy of the kindness of strangers (and, of course, my traveling companions, both of whom had language skills that I lacked). At first, all those foreign tongues were a bit of a novelty (especially Italian out of the mouths of babes—and I don't mean the little guys), but what was at first fascinating and charming quickly became frustrating and overwhelming. I couldn't help but feel like I was only getting half the picture, like listening to music through only one headphone.

Now, have you ever laid out a tarot spread, taken one look, and thrown up your hands because you have *no* idea what the cards mean? You *know*, from instinct, study, and experience that the cards before you Mean Something; you know that there are messages in the ol' Mystical Inbox, waiting to be picked up and read. Because your instinct is to create order out of chaos, because your brain wants to be communicated to, it will try to suss out the patterns and rearrange symbols into something useful. But without a good grasp of the language, the house of cards descends into a jumbled mess and you're left feeling frustrated because you just . . . don't . . . get it.

The idea of tarot-as-language is perhaps one of the cornier metaphors around, the kind of thing you might find in the "fluffy bunny" tomes that drive most of the tarotists I know bananas. Be that as it may, for me it remains one of the most useful ways of thinking about tarot; I return to it constantly. The very first spread I laid out was "all Greek to me," as they say—indeed, I clearly remember that that very phrase came to mind. I furrowed my brow for a while, then had one of those "aha" moments that comes before breaking into laughter at myself (yes, the laugh came too). I'd learned a new language before; immediately, my course of study and the basic shape of the learning curve became clear. Before I could read, I would have to invest some time in the basics: a smattering of vocabulary, the essential parts of speech, rudimentary sentence construction. Immediately I could wrap my head around the problem and conceptualize it.

The foreign-language metaphor was a point of reference, a place to begin, and—most importantly—an orientation. I knew where I had to go. First stop, the basic parts of speech. What are they in the tarot deck? The Major/Minor Arcana division, for starters, then the four suits, then the ten pip cards and the four Court Cards.

Once I had the basic parts of speech under control, I could begin to build my vocabulary.

What do the cards mean? Every tarotist with a bit of experience understands the vastness (and perhaps the existentialist vibe) of this question. As a beginner, I hadn't learned enough to psych myself out. I began to gather basic meanings for each card, assembling my own keyword lists from various books. I also looked to the cards themselves. Thanks to the beauty and artistic intelligence of Pamela Colman Smith's work (not to mention the fact that she pretty much lays it all out for us in the Minors), I had quite visceral reactions to the images and was able to cull meanings from those, too.

With parts of speech and the very beginnings of vocabulary, I began to construct sentences in the form of readings. Once again, I stuck to the basics: one-card readings, three-card readings, a card a day. Simple phrases—just enough to read the signs in a foreign country or ask the natives for directions—but sentences all the same. Through these first attempts at communication, I began to learn how all of the parts work together. Tarot became a medium through which I could tell stories.

Like me, you've perhaps heard tarot described as a vast book—so vast, in fact, that it encompasses the entirety of the human experience. I'd imagine that to an outsider whose only experience with tarot is that of fortune-teller stereotypes and its portrayal in movies, that might seem a smidge overblown. But having worked with tarot for over a decade, the notion of tarot-as-book makes perfect sense. The blocks of language are all present and accounted for; from there, we can shape and twist them into whatever story, missive, message, or memo we need to get out into the world (or, as is more likely, those messages are addressed *to* us, in the form of a "random" reading).

If we are to understand what the tarot says (and if we are to communicate those messages to another person), we must be equipped with a vocabulary. In the beginning, our vocabulary will be a hair's breadth away from English, perhaps; maybe little more than the equivalent of "yes," "no," and "check, please." But rudimentary must give way to rich if we are to receive what tarot has to offer. To really go deeper, we must constantly add to the stores.

The good news is that it doesn't take much to start building a tarot vocabulary. If you work with tarot at all, be it for readings or meditation or whatever, you'll pick things up and learn as you go. But I believe that it's really important to stretch yourself when it comes to vocabulary building, to make it an ongoing, conscious exercise and not something that "just happens." When you actively seek out new "words" for your tarot vocabulary, interesting things begin to happen. My friend and teacher Wald Amberstone calls this tapping into "layers of meaning." You'll be in the middle of a reading, and all of a sudden you'll start to make connections that you've never made before. Something completely random—and totally germane to the issue at hand—will pop into your head. Your right brain will start working overtime. Things will come out of your mouth that you never would have said in a similar reading six months previously. Your querent will say things like, "Yes, that's exactly it!" or "It's like you read my mind!"

You'll feel more confident, relaxed, and secure in front of the cards. You'll have ammunition. You'll be on solid ground. Most importantly, you'll have fewer of those "what the?!?" moments.

I've found the following sources and practices useful for building my vocabulary:

Know your archetypes. Here's where we get down to brass tacks. In my humble opinion, coupled with readings, *the* most important thing you can do to improve your tarot know-how is to work those archetypes to the bone. Know 'em like you know your own history. Identify them in the deck (don't forget that they're all over the Minor Arcana, too), then go out and learn as much about them as you can. Work with sources that have nothing to do with tarot. Look for them in your everyday life and learn how to identify them when you see them "in the wild." In a previous edition of this journal, I talked about "Tarot Hide and Seek," an exercise that involves actively looking for whatever turned up in your card of the day; it's great for building your archetype reserves, too.

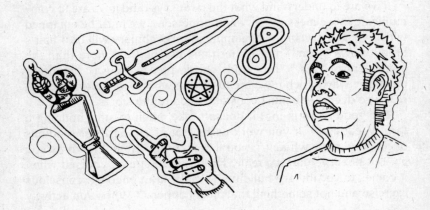

Read books on mythology, including books on non-Western myths. Read tons of stories, paying attention to the players, settings, and, most importantly, patterns in your reading over time.

Queen ◦ Swords

The Queen of Swords from *The Victoria Regina Tarot*

Know your symbols. That's another important thing you can do for your tarot practice. A good deck will be loaded with symbols, and all of those symbols are keys to a possible interpretation. Closely examine the cards in your deck and make notes of their symbols, then learn as much as you can about them. Invest in a good reference book or two and look them up. Compare your findings to your own personal symbolism; you'd be surprised how much knowledge of symbols you can pick up just from the business of living and socialization.

Sometimes, a single symbol on a single card is the key you need to unlock an otherwise perplexing reading. It's those readings (and they do come around) that remind me why vocabulary-building is well worth my time.

Take lots of notes. Your research on archetypes and symbols could fill notebooks all on their own. You may not want to separate them from your regular tarot materials, but be sure to include them somewhere.

Decks, decks, and—oh yeah—more decks. That compulsive tarot shopping streak can really earn its keep—if you take the time to actually work with the decks you buy (which is not always the point of buying new decks, I know, and of course that's okay). New decks mean new yummy symbols and new interpretations to consider. But beware! Remember that saying, "Garbage in, garbage out"? Be judicious about what you take in according to your own standards (not some blowhard who has decided that only certain decks and authors are "the only ones who get it right"). Personally, most of the time I like creative, well-researched decks that twist traditional meanings slightly but don't stray too far from them (I like to see things with a different pair of glasses, but I'd like to recognize what I'm looking at, too). Consider spending at least a little

◆ time with that little white book (or fat manual), but of course you
✳ can always let the cards be your guide (more symbols to study).
◆   **Books and classes.** These are obvious, but I'll mention them
50 here for completeness. Expose yourself to new ideas and perspectives on a regular basis.

An extensive vocabulary is one of the keys to tarot fluency. Have fun building yours!

Photo Tarot

by Mark McElroy

Do you long to create a personal tarot deck, but lack the skills to create your own illustrations? If so, why not express yourself with a Personal Photo Tarot (or PPT, for short)? With nothing more than a stack of photos and your own intuition, you can create a unique Majors-only deck in two hours or less.

Why Bother?
With thousands of attractive decks widely available, why bother to create your own?

First, creating a PPT encourages you to see too-familiar archetypes from a personal perspective. No matter how much you like the Empress in Nigel Jackson's *Medieval Enchantment* deck, seeing her with fresh eyes can be a challenge when drawing that card for the umpteenth time. But creating an Empress out of a photo of your mother prompts you to see the card in a new light and experience its energy in a different way.

When you create a PPT, you create a tarot deck that is uniquely yours. When reading for yourself, you will find the deck addresses your concerns with unusual directness. When reading for others, the fact that you've created your own deck will never fail to impress.

And, of course, creating a PPT provides you with an intimate way to "live the tarot." As you see the deck's archetypes reflected in moments from your own experience, you'll become a more fluent speaker of the oracle's visual language.

Creating the Basic Deck

Creating a PPT should entertain you for an hour or two—not a month or two. Resist the urge to spend weeks looking for just the right Temperance card. If you're willing to find images that are "good enough" and move on, you can create a PPT in three simple steps:

1) Choose the photos you want to use.
2) Match your images with Major Arcana archetypes.
3) Fill in "holes" as needed.

Choosing the Pictures

When you're ready to start, break out your pith helmet, whip out your binoculars, and pull on your khaki shorts. It's time to go on a photo safari!

Great personal photos are the heart of any PPT, and they can often hide where you least expect them. You'll be surprised how stealthy your most Arcana-worthy photos can be! Pry elusive photographic prey from between the pages of those expandable photo albums. Dig through the jungle of junk in your office. Acquire candidates from frames around your home—or even the homes of friends and relatives—with all the relentless vigor of a modern-day Indiana Jones. (Humming the theme song from *Raiders of the Lost Ark* while doing so is strictly optional.)

If you're a computer user with a digital camera, you'll be surprised at how many great digital photos are lurking on dusty CD-

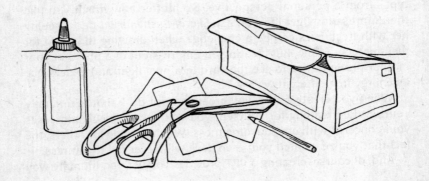

ROMs and in abandoned subdirectories on your computer's hard drive. Do a search on the file extensions most often associated with images: .jpg, .gif, .tif, and .bmp.

Rather than limiting yourself to twenty-two photos (one per Major Arcana card), gather up as many pictures as possible. At this point, avoid looking for specific images to match specific archetypes. Trust the universe to draw your attention to the snapshots you need.

Assembling the Arcana

With your plundered pictures scattered on the desktop, table, or floor, you're ready to assemble your Major Arcana. Once again, this process should be playful, not painstaking. While you *can* spend hours poking around for the perfect picture of your ex to use as the Devil, I suggest you avoid "perfectionist's paralysis" by employing any one of the following three methods.

Wheelin' and Dealin'

Wheelin' and Dealin' forces you to make speedy choices. Start by dealing the Major Arcana cards from your favorite deck into a large circle in the center of the floor. (On a computer, you can create twenty-two folders—one for each Major Arcana card—on your desktop.)

That done, examine each photo's subject, content, spirit, or energy and deal it onto the appropriate Major Arcana card (or, on a computer, just drag each photo to an appropriate folder). Spend no more than ten seconds with any one photo. This isn't a scientific process, so don't fuss too much over whether Aunt Edna should be the Priestess or the Pope.

Some cards will have multiple matches. (No problem! Arcana cards that attract huge piles of pictures are often soul cards, birth cards, or Majors representing an important theme for this life.) Some cards will have only one or two matches. (That's fine.) One or two Majors may wind up with no matches at all. (Don't worry. Later on, we'll make sure every Major finds a mate.)

Once you run out of pictures, it's time to move through the Major Arcana card by card, narrowing your options to one photo per trump. If you just can't decide which of three possible candidates should become your final Star card, let the universe choose for you: just close your eyes and pick a random photo.

Wheelin' and Dealin' is fast, fun, and intuitive, but it's also easy to be drawn into the photos themselves and lose sight of the goal. If

♦
✳ you feel you need a process with a little more structure, a method I
♦ call the Keyword Quest may be just the ticket.

The Keyword Quest
As before, deal out the twenty-two Majors or create twenty-two
folders on your computer's desktop.

That done, take a single sheet of paper and draw a line down the
middle, dividing it into two columns. In the left-hand column, list
the names of every Major Arcana card, from the Fool to the World.
In the right-hand column write down two or three keywords for
each Major card. For the Magician, for example, you might write,
"Capability, Focus, Empowerment."

Once you've defined keywords for each Major, root through your
photo pile, looking for pictures that correspond to the keywords
you've created. Remember that snapshot of your nephew straining to take his first steps? If you decide that photo makes a good
illustration for "Capability, Focus, and Empowerment," choose that
photo to be your Magician.

Once you make a choice, strike the corresponding Major Arcana
card off your list. While slow at first, this will get faster as you go.
For those who love checking items off to-do lists, this is probably
the best method for matching images to Arcana. For those who prefer to walk on the wild side, the Rite of Randomness is probably a
better choice.

The Rite of Randomness
When it comes to assigning a specific picture to a specific Major as
quickly as possible, the Rite of Randomness is hard to beat.

As before, deal the twenty-two Majors into a circle (or create
twenty-two folders on your desktop). Then, in a move that will make
Type-A taroticians squeal with rage, shuffle your face-down photos
and randomly deal one onto each Major card. (On a computer, you
can change your software to show filenames only—with no thumb-
nail images—and drag random files to the appropriate folders.)

That done, turn your photos over. Behold a Major Arcana like no
other: a pictorial sample of your life, generated by random universal forces! An exciting quest for meaning begins right away. What
does your labrador puppy have to do with Justice? How might your
college roommate embody the stoic authority of the Emperor? Why
would the universe choose a snapshot of last year's daffodils to
represent the concept of Death?

The results may shock, surprise, or even offend you—but I guarantee the Rite of Randomness will help you create a dramatically different PPT. And of course, if you don't like the outcome of this exercise, you can always substitute conscious choices for any random images.

Filling in the Holes

If you use either Wheelin' and Dealin' or the Keyword Quest to match images to the Major Arcana, you will likely have a trump or two that winds up without a corresponding photo. Never fear! There are at least two ways to fill in the holes and complete your PPT.

Begin by taking a long look at the "leftovers"—pictures you left unassigned. Would any of these work better if they were cropped or trimmed? Use sheets of white photocopier paper or black construction paper to mask out portions of the photo. That picture of a smiling baby looking up at a spinning mobile might make a perfect Sun card once the mobile is out of the picture. (Note: when heirloom photos are involved, I recommend working with photocopies, which are easy to crop, enlarge, or shrink as needed.)

If all else fails, try the Rite of Randomness to fill in your missing Majors. If you don't like the results, you can always shuffle your photos and try again.

When you've chosen twenty-two photos, be sure to keep some record of which photo you assigned to which trump. (In the middle of a divination, you don't want to wonder, "Was Uncle Allan the Tower or the Hanged Man?") I like to write tiny numbers directly on the back of the prints; you may prefer to create a stand-alone list of majors and card descriptions ("The Tower: Uncle Allan falling out of the magnolia tree").

Testing the Deck

With one photo selected for each Major card, it's time to test your PPT. At this stage, your deck likely consists of twenty-two photos of varying sizes and shapes. As a result, shuffling may be a challenge, and you may be able to distinguish one photo from another, even when the pictures are face-down.

To compensate, place your PPT in a soft cloth bag or cover scattered cards with a cloth. Choose a question and, by reaching into the bag or under the cloth, select a photo to use as a response. Spend several minutes allowing the photographic Major to speak to you, and you'll be rewarded with a uniquely personal insight!

Tips and Suggestions

• If you have the negatives or files on hand, consider having inexpensive 3 × 5 prints made of the twenty-two photos you select. A uniform deck is easier to shuffle and conceals the identity of each card until you're ready to reveal it.

• To make your deck look more professional, consider mounting each photo to sturdy card stock, then trimming the corners with scrapbooking shears. To make the cards more durable, you can laminate them.

• If you're computer savvy, you can work with scans and digital photos to create a professional-looking PPT in record time.

• Photoshop Elements and other inexpensive photo editing packages provide a number of effects and filters you can use to enhance the images on your cards with a single click of the mouse.

• Most office supply stores carry a variety of card stocks made especially for use with home printers. Use sheets of perforated business cards to create a "mini" deck, or print your images on sheets of 3 × 5 index cards or 4 × 6 postcards.

• Missing a photo for a card? Grab your camera and snap an appropriate image. Ready for a bigger challenge? Dedicating yourself to shooting the "Tarot of My Trip to Mexico" will not only produce a PPT, it'll make your vacation slides a heck of a lot more interesting.

• PPTs make great presents. Long after your best friend will tire of Madonna's latest CD, she'll treasure the hand-made PPT you gave her for her twenty-first birthday. And remember: any PPT can quickly be converted to a great photographic calendar or coffee table book!

Even without an ounce of craftiness or artistic skill, in less than two hours you can own an heirloom PPT with a voice that's uniquely yours. Liberate your photos from those suffocating albums! Free them from their frames! It's time to put them to work generating the ideas and insights that only a Personal Photographic Tarot can offer.

The Magician

Practical Applications

Tossing Tarot

by Kevin Quigley

This was going to be an interesting reading, I could just feel it. The seeker sitting next to me was a curious bundle of energy. Very conservative, even staid, on the exterior, but everything else about this person was bubbling over as if ready to break out of some cocoon. After a few minutes of polite conversation, the feeling only increased. With a calm, controlled voice, my client spoke of living a rather pedestrian life until recently when a certain metaphysical experience had awakened a dormant yearning to connect with the deeper aspects of living a spiritual life.

Now, before I continue, this article is not about that client's experience, nor is it about this particular reading in any specific context. That is another's story to tell. Yet I feel that these kinds of events—the "lightning bolts" that reveal our greater aspects—often boil outward to have a ripple-effect on those we encounter. This article is about how I was affected by this person's remarkable ripple.

I am a musician as well as a tarot reader, and I've found a certain resonance between these two sides of myself. Over the past twenty years I've been drawn more and more to improvisational forms—away from a very structured classical beginning. It began with an interest in jazz and blues. Reading tarot has always struck me as an exercise similar to soloing in jazz. In both activities, one's job is to find and steer a nuanced, yet truthful, course through a familiar framework. In jazz you have the chord changes and a melody or *head* to hang on to. In tarot you've got a known set of images and a spread. What you say or what you play—your interpretation—is where the artfulness lies.

But the music that is closest to my heart is known as free improvisation. It strips away all structure and leaves only *play*. To me, this is the truest form of musical expression, attached only to the moment without contrivance or convention. It is to this free space that my tarot reading leapt when gently bumped by the ripple sent forth from my client's breakthrough experience.

We had set out to do a normal reading; a simple three-card spread was all we had time for. The cards were shuffled and cut. I drew the first one from the top of the deck, and as I prepared to place it on the table before us I caught a glimmer of anticipation in my client's eye. In it I saw hope for a message of reassurance and release, and that was my lightning bolt. Instead of placing the card in its prescribed position, I paused. My hand drifted below the surface of the table. I said, "I'm going to do something a little different" without knowing what that was exactly. And quickly, I flung three cards up into the air—zing, zing, zing!

There they landed, the Ten of Cups off toward the middle of the table. Closer to us were two cards face-down, one overlapping the other. Now, I know many jazz improvisers who speak of soloing as "having something to say." If you don't have something to say or have said what needs to be said, it's time to step out. In teaching free improv to other musicians, I've found that to be a useful idea, but I've modified it a bit. With everyone improvising together, all those statements can quickly compound into a cacophonous mess. Rather, it works better to ask questions than to make statements. A question leaves space for someone else to respond. And when possible, why not respond to the question of another with one of your own?

This is what these three cards on the table did for me—brought me to ask questions: of myself and of my client. "Why is that card so far away from all the others?" She knew the answer immediately. "That's my life in the 'real' world. That's my work and my family. It's all wonderful, but it's not connected to this other stuff. That's mine. I keep it private." The rest of the reading continued in this fashion, an intuitive and collaborative conversation. It felt as though the two face-down cards were being kept private, as they were sort of huddled together and staying close to us. And the cards began to ask questions of us. "Is this picture of the way things are one you'd like to maintain or one you'd like to alter?" "Are there any changes to be made?" "What are the aspects of life now that may be hidden even to us?"

We had made the leap into free improv, and it took us places that I doubt any spread with prescribed positions would have been able to. We weren't just tackling a problem or looking at an issue as simply something to be dissected, figured out, and wrapped up in a neat little package, but as a mystery to be entered into with a sense of play and reverence. When no predetermined form is present, form itself becomes an organic, evolving being that can hold just as much information as the individual cards. I have had the opportunity to explore a bit with this style of reading, and I would love to share some tips on how you might add it to your tarot toolbox as well.

First and foremost, remember that this is an intuitive style of reading. Because it is free-form, one needs to be as relaxed as the Fool, ready to step in any direction. Trust yourself and trust in the moment. When analyzing the way the cards have landed, things will pop into your mind: "Gee, the way that card rolled end-over-end, it looked like it was trying to escape from something!" Do not dismiss these valuable musings. Be on the lookout for them and incorporate them into your reading.

Secondly, I find it helpful to keep things quick and simple in terms of set up. Just toss the cards up into the air. I do generally try to hit the table, but I don't aim. The whole point is to trust in chance; cards are amazing things in the way they spin and whirl. I say, "Let them dance!"

Thirdly, while Tossing Tarot does work well with a large number of cards, fewer cards are most definitely best to begin with. Three appears to be the perfect starting number—enough cards to create some interesting relationships without becoming too confusing. If you need more information at any point in the reading, don't hesitate to fling some more.

Lastly, here are some things to consider:

Grouping: With three cards there are three possibilities. Generally, two cards will feel grouped and the other will be more independent or isolated. Less commonly, each will seem to be out on its own. Occasionally they will all land together. Also, consider the nature of their grouping. Do they feel like a tight-knit, well-ordered cluster of friends, or are they squabbling? Do they seem to be pushing each other away or trying to come together? I try to approach this concept before I take into account card meanings and images, so as to get the purest impression of grouping first. Then, later, I'll combine these impressions with what the cards actually are.

Distance: Take into account how far away each card has landed from the main surface. Do the more distant cards feel as though they are doing their best to remain unreachable, or might they perhaps represent some distant goal? Are the closer cards crowding or distracting you, or are they familiar and comfortable? Often, several factors may combine to give you a sense of a card's "attitude." Its final angle or flight path—did it spin all over the place or just pretty much drop into place?

Visibility: This begins with whether a card lands face-up or face-down, but can go beyond that. Did a card land on the floor, under the table, in the drapes? Did a card land over another card? Are the overlapping cards face-to-face, back-to-back, or facing the same way—up or down? How much do they cover each other? Is the covering card smothering the covered card or protecting it? Maybe even trying to coax it out into the light?

Level and Context: I also like to consider how the cards actually landed—and on or near what. Are they all flat on the table? Is one of them slightly propped up on a book at an angle? Did one make it into a nearby plant or close to a glass of water? Did it land on a person or touch something in the air? Did one land on fabric, one on wood, and one on paper? Any of these details can turn out to be the one that turns the key for the reading. As always, trust your intuition. If you feel that little tug of connection, it's worth remembering, if not mentioning.

Pattern: A final thing I look for in any reading, tossed or not, are patterns within the lay of the cards. Are there a surprising number of Sevens or Cups? Did they all land face-down? Do they all feature women? Is there an overwhelming color or shape? I use these patterns to give me a general "lay-of-the-land" for the reading. If I see a lot of Swords, that tells me something very specific. A lot of red might indicate something else.

Most often, a couple of these details will seem important right away. The ones that seem to jump out at you are a great place to begin. As you weave your way into the reading, other aspects will seem to fall into place to support this or that interpretation. Yet with this technique I've found that holding back at first can yield amazing results. You might want to consider simply asking the seeker a question about a detail you find particularly interesting. If you notice a strong reaction to any card, that's also a nice place to start. "I see, way across the table, the Four of Discs has landed next to the window sill. I wonder what it could mean. It's sort of propped up and almost facing back at us. What do you think?" Sometimes, you'll get an answer right away—and that answer can often lead you in a direction you would never have taken on your own. Sometimes, you may need to explain a bit about the meaning of the card itself before the conversation gets started, but once it does you'll find that a collaboration can develop between the reader and querent that can flex and flow in an almost musical way. You are improvising. You've found the *groove*.

Many improvising musicians, myself included, feel that the best play comes through when you've reached that magical point where you're able to suspend the judgments and choices made by an active and controlling ego. It is a mystical place where you simply become a conduit for the truth to pass right on through, unfiltered. The intuition leads. What seems important *is* important. The path is zigzag and clarity is reached gradually. There is no plan, there is no need for one. There is no structure but that which makes itself apparent. This to me is the essence and wisdom of the Fool. I say, "Why not bring that into the reading itself?" Trust and follow like the Fool. Read tarot like the Fool. Make Foolish music. Play.

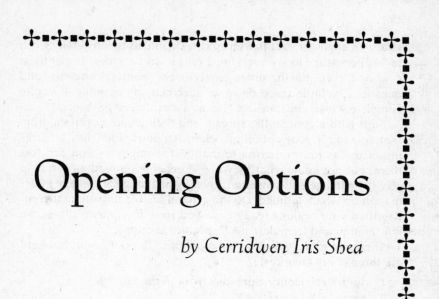

Opening Options

by Cerridwen Iris Shea

The tarot is not merely a tool for probing your subconscious; it is a way to open options that you might not consciously recognize. You need to be open to ideas outside your normal frame of reference, and tarot is a way to shake things up in the best possible way. However, that doesn't mean it will always be comfortable. Before you try to open your options with a tool as powerful and as forthright as the tarot, let go of preconceptions. Don't try to manipulate the cards into giving you the answer that you think you want; listen to what the cards actually have to say.

Specificity in the questions is important. A question as vague as "What should I do?" or "What's going to happen?" will get you an equally vague answer. A yes-or-no, one-card question could cut you off from the deeper aspects you need to know in order to make an informed decision.

Take your time in coming up with the questions. Ask too many questions, and you'll wear yourself out without getting all the information. Ask too few, and you're turning a blind eye to what you might need to know.

How do you know what to ask and how much to ask? By working on questions ahead of time. Write out your concerns. Take a few days to write detailed journal entries or letters to yourself, your guardian angel, or your patron spirits. Go into as much detail as you feel is necessary to lay everything out. Read back over the entries, over and over, making notes on recurrent themes, concerns, and questions. Whittle these down as succinctly as possible. If you're completely lost, you can say, "I'm at a loss. I need guidance."

Start with a general life spread, and then create questions from that spread for your option questions. Opportunities may be lurking in the astral, preparing to manifest. Sometimes you can feel them, but not know what they are. A general life reading can help give them image and sensation, giving you a tangible piece of information on which to build. Do the general life reading on a different day than your options reading, so you have the time to digest the information and formulate new, specific questions.

There are many ways to "open options" through tarot, but here are three of my favorites:

1. Multi-Deck Option Spreads ("Fork in the Road")
2. Question-by-Question
3. Question-by-Question with Build-ons.

Multi-Deck Spreads

I call this the "Fork in the Road" spread. You can use it to examine several choices at once by designating a different deck for each option, and one deck for the "unknown" option, and then laying out a line of cards for each choice. You use separate decks because some of the same cards may need to come up more than once, and you'll have to weigh their meanings in relation to the overall whole.

Let's say you're faced with a decision, and you have three options to choose from. You use four different decks (one for each choice, and one for the "unknown").

You decide how many aspects of each option you want to explore, and pull a card for each of them. (The cards should be pulled in the same order for each choice, so make sure you write down the positions in order—in the heat of the moment, you might forget.) For instance, if you want to know how each choice affects your environment, home life, family life, love life, finances, obstacles, opportunities, and the possible outcome, you'll pull a total of thirty-two cards: eight cards each from four separate decks, for the four choices in front of you.

That's a lot of cards, so if you want something a bit simpler, you can pick one card each for the mind, body, and spirit aspects of each choice. That's only three cards per possibility instead of eight.

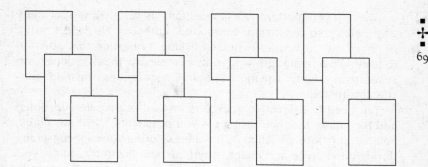

This is one of the few spreads in which I use a significator card. In order to find your significator card for the overall spread, go through each deck and choose the card that you feel most strongly represents you at that moment. (Forget anything you've been told as to which Court Card you are: in this exercise you can pick any card in the deck.) Take the chosen cards from each deck, shuffle them, and place them facedown. Pick one card. This is your significator card for the reading. The other cards are returned to their respective decks (in case they need to turn up elsewhere in the reading) and the spread begins.

Designate each deck to a particular option *after* you choose a significator, and designate one deck as the "unknown" deck. Now do the spread—and take notes, because you'll receive more information in this spread than you can retain. There's a popular theory that you'll retain information that's important and relevant; however, while you may retain information to which you connect most directly *at that moment*, there will be plenty of other information that will not make sense until days, weeks, or even months later. A set of good notes, or maybe even photographs, will have enormous value in the future.

I find the ability to compare the same positions in various options enormously helpful. Comparisons and contrasts lead me to more questions and a deeper thought process. I start looking at aspects of options in different ways, and I am able to make a more informed decision.

Question-by-Question
You can also work through your options with a single deck, one question at a time. You can ask several questions regarding each option or one question per option—however you feel it suits your needs.

Again, it is important to ask questions as simply and succinctly as possible. No complex or compound sentences. No "and," "but," or "however." If you find yourself asking a question that adds on to itself like a hydra, growing in its complexity, break it down into separate questions. The more specific the questions, the more specific the answers.

You need to ask active questions instead of passive questions, and remember that the tarot gives you possibilities, not absolutes. You are not "fortune-telling." You are exploring your subconscious through archetype and image. Anything you like in a reading, you can make happen through positive action. Just because a "good" card turns up doesn't mean the good will come to pass. It could come to pass if you take the appropriate action. The flip side of the equation is that if something negative turns up in a reading, you have advance warning. You can take the actions necessary to reach a different outcome. If you choose not to take action (yes, passivity is a choice) remember that, all around you, people are making active choices. As their personal universes bump your universe, there is the potential for change that will affect you, but in which you have chosen not to participate.

Which spreads should you use for your questions? Trust your instinct for each question. I find that if I use the same spread for question after question, I end up with mush. But if I use a Celtic Cross for one, a Medicine Wheel for another, and a Mind/Body/Spirit for a third, I receive more clarity.

Also, when you feel yourself tire, stop. Don't push through. Take a break and ask additional questions after you've rested. Information overload is not going to help.

Question-by-Question with Build-ons

As you work through your questions, you might have a question on a particular card within that question. There are several ways to handle that.

One way is to take the confusing card and use it as the basis for another spread. For example, in a Celtic Cross spread, the Ten of Wands comes up in the third position, Aspirations. Why would I aspire to feeling overburdened? Am I somehow sabotaging myself? Especially if the card seems not to make sense in the context of the rest of the reading, it's a good one on which to build for greater understanding.

I take the Ten of Wands and put it in the first position in a new Celtic Cross spread in order to clarify it. Or I would use it as the center card (spirit) in a Medicine Wheel spread.

Another way I could clarify the card is to draw an additional card or two with the specific intent to explain the Ten of Wands. I could pull the additional card or cards from the same deck, use a different deck, or even use a different type of oracle. I find runes and ogham sticks especially useful in clarifying tarot cards. Only pull one or two cards, though—any more, and it's time for a new spread, with the Card of Confusion at the center.

Take a few days after the reading to let the information sink into your bones and your soul. Don't feel that, two hours after your reading, you have to make life-changing decisions. Think about everything you've learned. Weigh the possibilities against each other. Is what you think you wanted really the best option, or has something else you never thought of appeared? Trust your gut beyond anything else. Your head and heart will lead you down the most complicated, convoluted roads possible. Your gut will lead you to your truth. After a few days, go back and re-read your notes. See if your frame of reference has changed at all. Then start writing journal entries about actions you can take in your decision-making process.

Readings are no good without implementation. You can read and read and read, gaining all kinds of information, but if you don't do

anything with it, it's a waste of time. Information is like a lump of dough: it needs to be shaped and baked, not left to rot.

Tarot is a tool. The more actively you use it, the more options you can open. If you use it as an excuse rather than an option, it will backfire. But used with intelligence and respect, it can help lead you to your best options.

Fooling Fortune

by Janina Renée

Although tarot readers emphasize the positive aspects of the cards in a reading, there is no getting around the fact that the appearance of certain cards is alarming because of their potential predictions of bad things to come. Here, let me interject that, as someone who has written four books on tarot, I am certainly interested in prediction; however, I do not believe in such a thing as inexorable Fate—just in the tendency of our attitudes and habits to take us down certain roads, and our actions to invite certain reactions. Although karmic factors come into play, some bad karma can be mitigated or outrun. I also allow for genuine randomness and fortuitous turns of events.

With these principles in mind, we may note that finding ways to improve one's luck and change one's path of destiny has always been a concern of folk magic, so many magical principles can be used to turn things around when you get a disturbing tarot reading—likewise if you have been experiencing a sense of foreboding or a run of bad luck. Here, imagery from the Fool, the Hanged Man, and the Death cards can suggest folk magic techniques for disrupting fixed energy, thought, and behavior patterns and getting out of the negative feedback loops that make for bad luck.

The Fool's Bag of Tricks

Sometimes the Fool denotes an innocent bungler, but in folklore, fools can also be tricksters. The Trickster archetype can be both clever and foolish, or cleverly foolish, or foolishly clever, and in so behaving, he sometimes baffles the decrees of fate.

In many magical traditions, a person experiencing troubling thoughts or negative energies can deflect them by playing the Fool.

Fool-type absurdities can include tricking supernatural forces by behaving like an animal, using nonsense words, dressing outlandishly, wearing masks or costumes—even cross-dressing—or taking on a nickname (often something ridiculous, so evil spirits won't bother with you). Along with these are many "reversal" actions such as talking backward, putting one's clothes on backward or inside-out, or standing on one's head or turning somersaults. Disruptive behaviors such as noisy pranks, acrobatics, water squirting, and telling obscene jokes are also part of the Fool's repertoire, as are childish behaviors such as playing with toys, skipping or swinging, and other youthful amusements. Some of these antics can be performed on the spur of the moment, (e.g., walking backward ten paces or turning your shirt inside-out), while others might be acted out during a period of ritual clowning. Reversal holidays like Halloween and Carnival can allow entire populations to rejuvenate themselves in this manner.

Indeed, anything that provokes laughter is part of the Fool's repertoire, and laughter is magically protective for a great number of reasons, including the fact that when we laugh, we show our teeth.

The Hanged Man's Perspective

XII The Hanged Man
El Colgado

The Hanged Man from *The Tarot of the Dead*

Some of the reversal actions associated with the Fool can also apply to the Hanged Man, for, by breaking up one's trend of thought, they promote new ways of seeing (which is one interpretation of this card). Many societies use the act of ritual reversal to overturn ordinary reality, gain insight, reverse time, and establish sacred space. For example, Congo magicians perform cartwheels and walk on their hands as a way of walking in the otherworld. Reversals can also provide a glimpse of the mythical world, as in the case of some Inuit groups who hold that people walked on their hands in the Original Time, before Raven turned the world upside down (establishing our present condition).

Another way to emulate the Hanged Man is to take a "time out." To the extent that you are able, suspend some of your activities, plans, and obligations to other people. It would be good if you could experience a period of doing nothing but carrying out the most basic requirements of work and life. If you can get away on vacation, go to a place that is very different from what you would normally choose. This is something that creative people do to provoke new insights and that shamans prescribe to effect healing; it also ties in with the spiritual practice of pilgrimage. However, don't have any expectations that anything special will happen. If nothing does happen to give you new perspectives, that is okay. You can return to your daily routine, trusting that changes are at work on an unconscious level.

Another meaning of the Hanged Man is sacrifice. People seeking to change their luck have traditionally entreated the gods or spirits with votive offerings, which are tokens given as a pledge to fulfill a vow in exchange for spiritual aid, or as thank-offerings for wishes granted. (In keeping with Hanged Man symbolism, votives can take the form of objects suspended from trees; in Greco-Roman society, these were often in the form of masks, puppets, and different types of pendants.) Another type of sacrifice is the give-away, which is a practice of the Plains Indians and others, where people hold or attend a gathering where they give away a large number of personal goods. In the most extreme cases (such as great misfortune or life-threatening illnesses), a person might give away everything that he or she owns. This was a custom among some Jewish and Inuit groups, such as the Padlimiut band of Caribou Inuit, who held that "whoever would invoke the Great Spirit must have no possessions save his breath." However, that is just one spiritual viewpoint. If you decide to make some sacrifice, you have to consider what level of sacrifice would be appropriate to your own situation.

Death and Transformation Rituals

The things that the Death card represents are intrinsic to many processes of transformation. This idea is represented in older versions, which showed not just a dry skeleton but decomposition, as well as growth in the form of sprouts emerging from the earth.

Many traditional societies have rituals that help ailing or unlucky individuals renew themselves by taking them through a symbolic death and transformation. The ritual death phase may involve giving away all of one's belongings (as mentioned above), or being symbolically dismembered by dancers with monster masks, or by lying in a grave or a coffin or wrapped in a shroud while funeral rites are read. The renewal phase may involve burning one's old clothes and donning new ones, or taking on a new name, or crawling through an arch of boughs or between the legs of a woman, or re-entering the house through a hole opened in the roof, or even by being given a new set of parents. The purpose of these actions is expressed in a Jewish renaming ritual from the 1600s: "If death has been decreed for [name], let it not be fulfilled. Now he is a different person, like a new human being, a child just born."

In ordinary everyday tarot readings, the Death card is likely to point to endings and beginnings in more mundane affairs, so it might be a bit of overkill to put on an elaborate ritual or make other drastic changes in response to it. However, you can symbolically take yourself through the transformation process.

After considering whatever advice your reading has offered, lay out the Death card, followed by your significator card, the Judgement card, and the World card. Then say, "I, [name], son/daughter of [name parents], acknowledge that I have made a break with the past. Now am I renewed into a life of happiness and wholeness." If you would like to go to extra effort, you could reinforce the symbolism by first putting your significator into a little box and burying it in the ground, then resurrecting it for the tarot rite.

At this point, we can see how many other tarot cards and readings can prompt theatric ritual gestures for changing one's luck. For example, the World could suggest a new spin on the old Scandinavian custom of dancing out the trolls. The Tower could suggest the Voodoo practice of overturning a cup, or the old Indian and Babylonian custom of breaking pots to disperse bad influences. Interestingly, the physical motions and sensations of breaking crockery are said to be very therapeutic. Cups, bowls, and plates might also be overturned or broken as a way of releasing issues and anxieties associated with different Cups and Pentacles cards, while for Swords and Wands issues you might practice some knife-throwing or arrow-shooting, which are also traditional protective practices (assuming you have a nice outdoor space where you won't endanger anyone). Even people who don't believe in magic may be able to appreciate how these dramatic actions can give a person a sense of relief and a refreshed outlook.

Elements of Tarot

by Nina Lee Braden

While I love using candles, crystals, incense, chimes, and other tools to mark a time and space apart for special work, I have found that using the four Aces of a tarot deck is all that is necessary. Tarot, in its wonderfully vivid flexibility, gives us several exciting ways to explore the four alchemical elements of fire, water, air, and earth. Perhaps the most obvious way of exploring the elements is through the suits of the Minor Arcana. In different decks and systems, each suit has been paired with each element, but perhaps the most widely accepted correspondence is Wands for fire, Cups for water, Swords for air, and Pentacles for earth. But no matter what system (or systems) you use, tarot makes a clear representation of the elements.

When I do ritual work, study, or meditation, I like to use tarot for representations of the elements. Normally, I use the four Aces. I have used the Aces in a variety of methods: placing them in the four directions to be visual foci for the elements, carrying them around the ritual or meditation space as tools for cleansing and protecting the area, and setting them on an altar to indicate the four directions. One simple method I use is to pick up each Ace and walk clockwise around the space, saying, "I ask for the blessing and protection of the element of [appropriate element for the Ace being held]." At the end of my working, I go counterclockwise and in reverse order and say, "I thank the element of [element] for its blessing and protection."

As I walk the circle, I like to visualize colors forming a protective sphere. I begin with Wands/fire in the east, and visualize red flames forming around the circle as I walk it holding the Ace of Wands up high. I next use the Ace of Cups for water in the south, and I visualize blue waves washing the circle. Then I'll visualize a yellow force field of solidified air forming as I walk the circle carrying the Ace of Swords from the west. Finally, I'll go to the north, and walk the circle carrying the Ace of Pentacles and visualizing a brown earthen wall.

I realize that my element/direction correspondences are different from what many people are used to, and if you decide to try this for yourself, please use the direction/element correspondences that you are used to.

I usually open my tarot classes with a simple ritual so that all of us will feel focused and will respect the classroom as space of serious (and yet often fun) study. It is truly a space away from our normal lives, and using a short ritual to start class helps to set the class apart from our normal routine. For the first variation, I'll ask each student to separate his or her Aces from the rest of his or her deck. I'll hold up my Ace of Wands and say, "We ask for the blessing of fire . . ." and each student, going clockwise around the room, will hold up his or her Ace of Wands in rhythm and repeat, "Fire." We do this in turn for all four Aces. It takes only a couple of minutes, but we have used the four Aces to bless the classroom. We each use our own decks, our own Aces, and it is truly exciting to see the variety of cards bringing in the elements with different subtle differences. At the end of the class, we do the same thing in reverse, going counterclockwise with one difference. We hold up each Ace, and as we go around the circle, saying, "I thank the element of [element]," we lower our Aces, one by one.

Another variation is for group work in a large space, either outdoors or in a large room. I choose four people to hold large Aces (around 8 × 10 inches). Each person goes to the appropriate direction. Each person in the circle has his or her own Aces out. The person in the east with the large Ace of Wands will hold it aloft, and everyone will line up behind the carrier of the Ace of Wands. The carrier will face east and say, "We ask for the purification, blessing, and protection of fire" and begin to walk around the space clockwise. Everyone will follow, raising up his or her Ace when he or she passes the east. After each person has gone around the circle for one full rotation, the person assigned to carry the Ace of Cups from the south will raise it up, saying, "We ask for the purification, blessing, and protection of water" and begin to walk the circle. Again, each person in the space will walk clockwise around the area, raising the Ace of Cups in salute as he or she passes the south. The other two directions/elements are treated the same way. At the end of the class or ritual or other group work, the same thing is done in reverse, giving thanks to each element.

After two and a half years of using the Aces in this manner, I decided to try a couple of alternative methods of using the tarot to set aside time and space. The first method uses the Court Cards. For me, Kings represent fire, Queens water, Knights air, and Pages earth. If you use a different method, feel free to adapt this to work with your system. Combining the elements of the suits and the elements of the Court Card ranks, we can think of the King of Wands as fire of fire, the Queen of Cups as water of water, the Knight of Swords as air of air, and the Page of Pentacles as earth of earth. This method works well, but there is a different feel to it. With the Aces, there is a purer and more abstract feel. With the Court Cards, there is greater focus or intensity. I normally use the Aces, but there are times when using the Court Cards might be preferred, especially if there is a desire to represent maturity (king and queen) and youth (knight and page).

Another way to use the Aces is to use the Major Arcana cards that represent the twelve signs of the zodiac. I normally use the four cardinal signs (Aries, Cancer, Libra, and Capricorn) because cardinal signs are initiating—they start things. However, there is also a valid argument for using the four fixed signs (Leo, Scorpio, Aquarius, and Taurus) because fixed signs are stabilizing and strengthening. I use the correspondences of the Builders of the Adytum, which are an updated version of the Golden Dawn correspondences. In this system, using

ACE OF STAVES

The Ace of Staves from *Medieval Enchantment: The Nigel Jackson Tarot* the cardinal signs, Aries is the Emperor and would be fire in the east. Cancer is the Chariot and could be water in the south. Libra is Justice and would be air in the west. Capricorn is the Devil and would be earth in the north. If you choose to use the fixed signs, you could do so, and have Leo and Strength for fire, Scorpio and Death for water, Aquarius and the Star for air, and Taurus and the Hierophant for earth.

There is an alternative way to use the Major Arcana as a visual aid in ritual, study, or meditation space. If you are familiar with the Pagan wheel of the year, you may know of the eight sabbats or holy days. You can use the cards corresponding to the four cardinal signs to represent the four holidays of the equinoxes and solstices, for indeed the four cardinal signs begin on these days. You can use the cards representing the four fixed signs for the four cross-quarter holidays of Beltane, Lammas, Samhain, and Imbolc. Your tarot wheel of the year would be Emperor (Spring Equinox), Hierophant (Beltane), Chariot (Summer Solstice), Strength (Lammas), Justice (Fall Equinox), Death (Samhain), Devil (Winter Solstice), and Star (Imbolc).

When I began my tarot studies, I used tarot for self-discovery and personal growth. Later, I began to do readings for others and to teach tarot. The more I study tarot and use it, the more ways I find to incorporate it into my life. Using tarot to help set aside time and space for spiritual work has been an exciting pathway in my tarot journey and in the journey of many of my traveling companions.

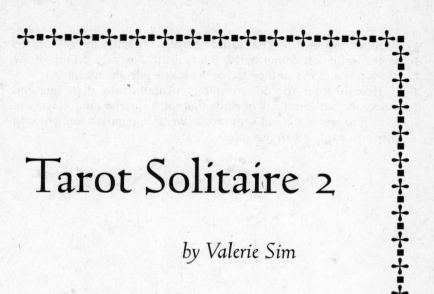

Tarot Solitaire 2

by Valerie Sim

This is Part Two of a series. For the full instructions and reading guidelines for the Klondike version of tarot solitaire, please refer to the 2007 Tarot Reader.

This version of solitaire is named Pyramid because of its triangular layout of twenty-eight cards. The object of the game is to eliminate the pyramid by finding pairs of cards totaling thirteen. Kings are counted as thirteen by themselves, and are removed singly. Queens have a value of twelve, and Jacks have a value of eleven. The pip cards are played as numbered. At the beginning of the game, only the cards at the bottom of the row are available for play. Higher rows in the pyramid become accessible as the cards below are removed. The cards not in the pyramid itself are put in a "stock" pile and cycled through one at a time. Unused cards from the stock pile are put in the "waste" pile faceup, so that the top card remains available for play.

The three areas of play are as follows:

Pyramid Tableau: The pyramid initially contains twenty-eight cards arranged in seven overlapping rows (see Figure 1). A card cannot be removed from the pyramid if it is covered by another card.

Stock/Waste Pile: The stock and waste piles, faceup, are located in the lower-left corner below the tableau. The card on top of the stock pile and the card on top of the waste pile are available.

Discard Pile: The discard pile is located to the right side and below the tableau. Pairs of cards that total thirteen (and Kings) are moved to this stack and kept facedown. The game is won when all fifty-two cards are in this pile.

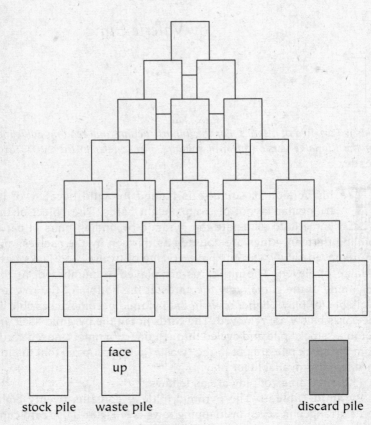

stock pile   waste pile

face
up

discard pile

Figure 1

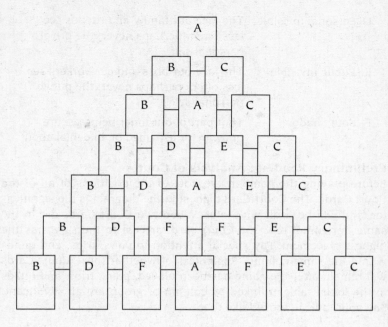

Figure 2

Seeing the Pyramid Tableau as a Spread

You will see from Figure 2 that the cards are grouped into columns, and labeled A, B, C, D, E, or F. These columns represent parts of a tarot spread. The cards in columns B and C represent aspects that can be seen or are apparent in the private and public sectors, respectively. Their counterparts, columns D and E, represent what is unseen, or less often seen, in those same sectors. Column A, in the center of the pyramid, corresponds to the soul or spiritual self, and column F, inside and partially surrounding the soul column, is read as the soul shadow.

A. Soul	The spiritual questing self, or soul
B. Personal visible	The face our family and friends know well
C. Public visible	The face seen by our boss, co-workers, and others we interact with publicly

D. Personal invisible	The face our family and friends see less often, perhaps never; the private personal self
E. Public invisible	The face our boss and co-workers see less often, perhaps never; the public personal self
F. Soul Shadow	That part of our inner being we are unaware or ashamed of, in denial about

Preliminary Reading: Analysis of Courts

Before playing the game, make note of the positions of all of the Court Cards. The Court Card highest in the diagram is the significator, and will be dealt with later. When two Court Cards are in the same horizontal row, the Court card farthest to the right has the highest placement. Pay special attention to pairs, trios, and quads within the same column. Regardless of whether these Court Cards will remain after the game has been played, pairs, trios, and quads in the initial tableau linked by column or group are all significant. Say your tableau looked like this:

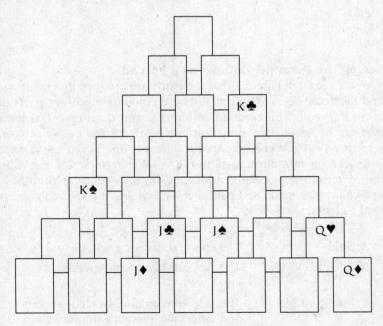

Figure 3

First, "translate" from playing cards to tarot cards: clubs = Wands, hearts = Cups, spades = Swords, diamonds = Pentacles. We have two Kings, but they are not in the same column. The King of Wands is the most elevated, and will become the significator in a supplemental reading (to be explained later). The King of Swords is not connected to the King of Wands, or to any other King by column, and is disregarded. We have two Queens (Hearts/Cups and Diamonds/Pentacles) in column C, the face publicly seen. This would indicate, whether these cards remain at the end of play or not, that there is a nurturing aspect to this person that is apparent to those with whom he or she interacts publicly. The Queens add a sensitive, perhaps mothering touch, which is witnessed by some or all co-workers, and/or by the supervisor. Extremely significant are the three Jacks, all of which fall into group F, or the soul shadow. This person may be in denial about certain immature behaviors that may be hurting him professionally, and/or he may unknowingly suffer from an "imposter syndrome," which causes him to always feel that he is not really as good as his achievements would indicate. He may be haunted by this, and fear that some day he will be "exposed."

Reading the Game Remainder: The Faces We Wear

Now, play the game according to the rules in the first paragraph. When you can go no further, consider the cards that remain at the end of play. For example:

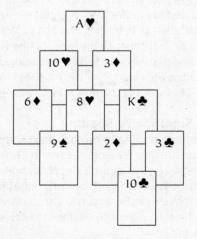

Figure 4

So, to recap, we have:

A. Soul	Ace of Cups and Eight of Cups
B. Personal visible	Ten of Cups and Six of Pentacles
C. Public visible	Three of Pentacles, King of Wands, and Three of Wands
D. Personal invisible	Nine of Swords
E. Public invisible	Two of Pentacles and Ten of Wands
F. Soul Shadow	No cards

Soul: Ace of Cups and Eight of Cups. Love and faith are very important to this person. He is probably quite spiritual. It is also likely, per the Eight of Cups, that he walks a rather solitary spiritual path, as opposed to a traditional or mainstream one. He may be somewhat of a loner or hermit.

Personal visible: Ten of Cups and Six of Pentacles. Others see a happy family life, and probably see this person as giving.

Public visible: Three of Pentacles, King of Wands, and Three of Wands. This person is viewed as a team player. He is passionate about his work and probably inspires others easily. Most would regard this person as both confidant and somewhat visionary. He is not afraid to think "out of the box."

Personal invisible: Nine of Swords. Here we see that this person has inner demons that are not readily apparent to all—perhaps not even to those who are closest to him. It looks like he has a tendency to "over think," and he may suffer from nightmares and/or insomnia.

Public invisible: Two of Pentacles and Ten of Wands. What the co-workers don't see is that this person feels like he has to juggle to get everything done, and that he often feels overwhelmed. Chances are that this will likely remain unseen due to the probable "imposter complex" described earlier, of which the querent may or may not be aware.

Supplemental Significator Reading

This is a mini-reading honing in on the Court Card identified earlier as the significator for this reading. Generally, I don't use significators in my readings. For this complex spread, however, I have found that the significator is a welcome and illuminating addition to the overall reading. These cards, and the cards drawn in the supplemental reading, help to identify possible roadblocks, and a way to move beyond them.

To do this supplemental reading, place the significator (here identified as the King of Clubs/Wands) in the middle of your reading surface. Shuffle the discard pile thoroughly and turn it face-down. Now, place the top card from the discard pile to the left of the significator, the next card underneath the significator, the third card to the right of the significator, and the final card above the significator. The layout looks like this:

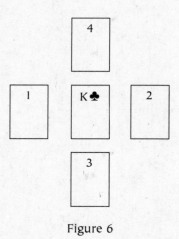

Figure 6

Assume the cards drawn are as follows:

1. What/where you have been: Five of Pentacles. Spiritually lost and/or impoverished? Or maybe just financially challenged and fearful. Could be either . . . or both.

2. What/who you are becoming: Ace of Wands. A new person, or an invigorated soul experiencing rebirth and new and fertile possibilities. The fear in the previous Five of Pentacles has been for the most part conquered, and a whole new outlook is glimpsed.

3. A strength not yet realized: Death. This card speaks of the ability, much like a snake, to shed the old and resurrect the new. Death grants the subject the ability to move on, to begin anew, even at difficult times. It is a great reinforcing card to the Ace just discussed.

4. A possible future impediment: Six of Cups. A tendency to cling to the past. Don't get stuck in "woulda coulda shouldas" or might-have-beens. Let the past hold lessons, but let go of distant heartaches.

I hope you have enjoyed this look at how solitaire and tarot can be wedded to illuminate the road we walk on this game of life. Live, learn, and don't forget to laugh.

Maiden, Mother, Crone

by Corrine Kenner

The ancient myth of the Triple Goddess—the Maiden, the Mother, and the Crone—has been told and retold for centuries. One of the most popular interpretations of the myth focuses on the maiden goddess Persephone, her mother Demeter, and Hecate, the crone who served as Persephone's companion, mentor, and guide.

According to legend, Persephone went out to pick wildflowers one day. As she reached down to pluck a particularly beautiful narcissus, Hades, lord of the underworld, reached up and pulled her down into his realm. There he forced her to become his bride.

Persephone's mother Demeter—crazed with fear, frantic with loss, and half-mad with grief—searched desperately for her lost daughter. No one seemed to know where the girl had gone. Persephone had literally vanished from the face of the Earth.

Finally, Demeter happened to meet the crone goddess, Hecate, who joined in the search. The two eventually met up with Helios, the Sun god. From his position in the sky, Helios had seen the abduction. He shed light on Persephone's whereabouts, and Hecate volunteered to travel into the underworld to help her.

Meanwhile, Demeter mourned. She was the goddess of grain and harvest, but while she grieved, life on Earth came to a standstill. Nothing grew, and the end of the world seemed imminent.

Finally, Zeus forced Hades to relinquish his bride—but not before Hades had tricked her into eating four pomegranate seeds. According to the rules, anyone who ate anything in the underworld could never be allowed to return to Earth; Hecate saved the day when she suggested that Persephone simply be compelled to return to Hades for part of each year. The gods agreed that Persephone would spend one month with Hades for each seed she had consumed. As a result, Persephone was allowed to spend eight months a year with her mother.

Each year, to this very day, the cycle repeats. When Persephone is away, in the dark and foreboding land of the dead, Demeter grieves and the earth grows cold. But when Persephone returns, Demeter—and Earth itself—springs back to life.

For thousands of years, women have identified with the Maiden, the Mother, and the Crone. The Triple Goddess is more than a myth, however: she's also a role model for tarot readers.

Here's how connecting with the triple goddess can help you bring your romance readings back to life.

Find Your Inner Maiden

The sheer joy and enthusiasm of the Maiden goddess is a welcome addition to any tarot reading. Just think back to the way you acted when you were a teenager, and you'll probably have a good sense for how the Maiden would act if she were giving a romance reading.

Decorate your room. Most teenagers plaster their rooms with posters and pages torn from magazines—all icons and symbols of idealized romance.

If you want to add some maiden energy to your romance readings, start by decorating your sacred space the way a maiden might. Light

pink or red candles to symbolize passion and romance. Instead of a standard significator, slide a real photo of a loved one—or a couple—into your spread. While you don't need to dredge up your old copies of *Teen Beat*, you're never too old to collect other odds and ends that symbolize romance. Try accenting your romance reading area with movie or theater tickets, champagne glasses, restaurant menus, or phone numbers scrawled on napkins from the local bar.

Show some enthusiasm. Teenagers love to talk. They love gossip, they love romantic intrigue, and they're passionate about sharing their secrets with a few trusted confidants. The next time you sit down to do a romance reading, set the high-level discussions aside, and prepare to dish instead.

Be willing to kiss and tell. Get into the habit of developing an interest in other people's romantic lives, even when you're not doing a tarot reading. Ask other people how they met their significant others. Ask what they find most attractive in a mate. Ask what they like to do on dates. Be open to your inner teen—and be open to hearing the details of other people's romantic pursuits.

Listen to Your Mother

Tap into the power of the Mother goddess, and your readings will be powerful, too.

Get into shape. Mothers give shape and form to their children: they literally provide a physical vessel for children to grow after conception, and then they provide a safe physical environment for children to grow up.

As a tarot reader, it's your job to offer a safe and comfortable physical environment for a reading—and to provide a structure and form for the reading itself. Check in with the Mother goddess for help when you choose decks, spreads, and focal points for every reading.

Nurture, comfort, and protect. Just as you should be able to trust your mother to keep your secrets, romance readers should always safeguard the feelings and the privacy of their querents. Nothing disclosed to you during a romance reading should ever leave the table.

Prepare for a few tears. Keep a box of tissues handy. Mothers and romance readers can both expect to spend some time consoling those who cry. It wouldn't hurt to have a few emotional Band-Aids in your purse, either.

Dust, if you must. Mothers spend years dealing with their family's filth. Unfortunately, dirty laundry is part of a romance reader's job description, too. Just remember to clean and clear your sacred space. If you do a mental sweep after every session, you can think of it as "light" housekeeping.

Go See Your Grandmother

While feminists work to reclaim the word "crone," you might find it easier to connect with the senior aspect of the goddess by thinking of her as a kindly old grandmother—and imagining all the wisdom and experience that she could bring to a tarot reader's table.

Be a good listener. Many people come to tarot readers because they want to talk—and nobody listens better than a grandmother does.

Turn to the Grandmother goddess for guidance when you need the time and patience to hear the whole story, without interrupting or second-guessing the teller.

Remember the past. Every grandmother was a maiden and a mother once herself—and every grandmother remembers what it was like to date, fall in love, and find herself a mother. Grandmothers have a lifetime of experience to draw upon when they connect with other people.

Be ready to hear anything. By the time most women are in their fifties, sixties, and beyond, they've heard hundreds of stories of love, betrayal, jealousy, and despair. They've even lived a few of those stories themselves.

Call the Grandmother goddess to your tarot readings, and you'll find that she's shockproof. There's nothing she can't handle.

Grandmothers have wise advice. Grandmothers know there's a fine line between giving advice and telling other people what they "should" or "shouldn't" do. During a tarot reading, the Grandmother goddess is a subtle guide to the message from the cards—with just the right suggestion or two offered from personal experience.

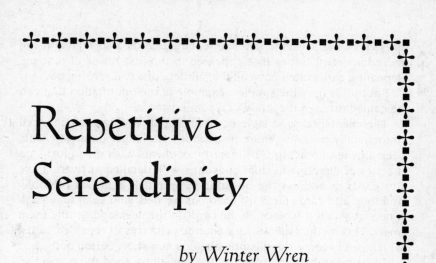

Repetitive Serendipity

by Winter Wren

When I sit down with an individual for a reading, I let her know up front that I will tell her what I see, not what she wants to hear. I may use polite ways of saying what needs to be said, but I will still say it. Not necessarily appreciating my direct honesty regarding some factors or the outcome in a reading, clients have sometimes asked me, "What if I were to shuffle the cards again? Would I get the same results?" Because of my own stubborn Taurean nature, I know it is easier to believe what is seen. It is likely I will shuffle several times, place the deck before them once more and let them try it. They are quite surprised to see some of the same cards appear again, often in the same position in the spread as they had been before. The cards that appear for the first time in this second spread usually allow me to give them even deeper details into their issues. I have never seen anyone ask for a third attempt.

Seeing the cards repeat in the second spread validates to the client the ability of the tarot to speak its own message. It removes doubts about the simple "randomization factor" influencing the reading. It is a way of showing querents that the message is not a chance turn of the cards or the reader's take on their life. It lends credibility to what was discussed and the choices that are now present in the seeker's life. The repeated cards also highlight the more important issues that appeared in the first round of reading. Repeating cards often have all the subtlety of a well-swung bat.

But that is only the simplest example of the information that can be gained through the study of repeating cards.

The client-preferred style of professional readings has changed dramatically over my tenure as a reader. No longer do most clients seek a general reading. The majority of clients wish me to focus on a series of direct, individual questions with detailed answers. I use five cards to address the question in as much depth as possible, and then add cards for clarification as needed. And each time I ask a new question, I replace all the cards in the deck and shuffle them anew. This method allows for numerous chances of repeated cards, which can become significantly obvious in a short period of time.

To gain the best information, the questions need to be specific: What does _____ need to know about _____? What is _____'s next step to achieve _____? What is standing in the way of _____? How will making this choice affect _____? I then fan the entire deck and have the client consciously select a card as I ask for each one specifically.

As I notice repeated cards appearing when reading in this manner, I begin making mental notes about the cards and the types of questions in which they appear. Often, after the third or fourth appearance, the seeker will make a comment about a particular card showing up over and over. If they do not, I will make mention of it to him or her.

At this point, I begin taking the reading to the next level. We begin to look at how the situations in the reading are interrelated. What common factors do they share? Is there a core problem causing

issues in more than one area of the seeker's life? Is this an issue that the seeker is actually aware of? How can this issue be addressed? What does the client need to know to better work with or eliminate this key factor? This process makes for a thorough and often intense reading session, which allows the client to take from the reading as much clear information about available choices as can be gained in one session.

Repetition in Action

A session might well look like the following: Eva settles in for a reading on career issues in her life. Her first question: "I want to advance in my career, yet I have been passed over for promotion twice in the last year. What is going on?" Focusing on "What is blocking Eva's career advancement?" I shuffle and then fan the deck, face-down. I ask Eva to choose a card to represent the heart of the matter—her career advancement. As she hands me the card, I position it face-down, careful to place it in the same orientation as it was when she drew it (this is important, as I read reversals). I then ask her to select two cards representing the obstacles to her advancement, and I place them on either side of the key card. Finally, I ask her to select two cards representing supports to her advancement, and I place those on the outsides of the previous cards.

Turning up the first card, we find the reversed Two of Swords, indicating that Eva is very much identifying herself with her career focus. Additionally, not advancing is having an effect on her identity at this time. Turning up the "obstacles" cards, we have the Nine of Cups and the Moon, both reversed. We now discuss her internal feelings about advancement: Is she counting on past work to get her there? Is this advancement what she really wants in her life? What does she see as her ultimate goal and is advancement the way to get there? If so, what additional steps should she be taking to achieve this? At this point, if things are not clear in her mind, I will have her draw three additional cards for further insight on the issue.

In Eva's case, she wants to know if she is having subconscious emotions that may be causing her to project some negativity toward advancement. She draws the upright Queen of Pentacles, the reversed Tower and the upright Empress. As we discuss these cards, Eva admits that her ultimate goal is to have her own business. She fears the changes and insecurity of creating her own business and leaving the directed world of her present career path. She feels she is a very good manager, but perhaps not as self-motivated as she would need to be to make a business succeed, whereas in the structured environment of her career, she knows what is expected of her.

Finally, we turn over the cards for the support Eva has in gaining advancement in her career, finding the reversed Knight of Cups and the upright King of Pentacles. Looking at these cards first as simple factors, we discuss what Eva sees as the emotional risks associated with her career advancement and what it might take to get her to leave her career and follow her heart. I also inquire whether these cards cause her to think of any specific people in her life connected to her career issues. The King of Pentacles reminds her of a senior manager who repeatedly tells Eva she should go out on her own and begin creating her own firm.

At this point, we proceed to her second question: "What is the best choice for me—staying in the corporate firm or starting my own business?" Focusing on this, I shuffle the entire deck again and ask Eva to choose a card to symbolize career for her. Then I ask her to choose a card for staying in the corporate arena and a second one for the result of doing so. With those placed, I ask her to choose a card for starting her own firm and a second one as the result of that choice.

For the card symbolizing her career, the upright Emperor appears. The card for remaining in the corporate job is the reversed Three of Pentacles and its resulting card is the upright Ten of Swords. The card for starting her own firm is the upright Empress and the upright Star symbolizes its results.

After discussing this, Eva poses her third question: "What steps do I need to take to start my own firm?" For the key issue, the upright Empress appears once more. The internal issues cards are the reversed Hermit and upright Ace of Pentacles. The external issues cards are the upright King of Pentacles and the reversed Ace of Wands.

The Empress card has appeared as the focal card in the last two questions in her reading. With this in mind, I enter into an in-depth discussion of all the aspects of the Empress card. Additionally, I point out that the upright King of Pentacles has now appeared twice in the position representing external supports in regard to her career choices. Eva expresses that she feels the King is definitely signifying her senior manager in this case. Her next question inquires as to whether or not this manager has a significant role in Eva starting her own firm. She was not extremely surprised when the King of Pentacles turned up in the key position for that question.

The long-term outcome of this situation had Eva starting her own firm and her former senior manager approaching her about a partnership situation. She felt the reading helped her identify her fears about starting her own business and recognize how her internal desire for her own business was contributing to her lack of advancement in her corporate position.

I firmly believe repeating cards are a wake-up call from the psychic realm. Lessons not learned are likely to be repeated in some form until they are learned. The same applies to repeated tarot cards. It is worth the time to investigate and understand the message being given.

The End of Your Rope

by *Elizabeth Barrette*

Most of the time when you do a card reading, you need something—usually starting with answers, or at least ideas that might help you figure out the answers. Sometimes, though, you *really* need something. Sometimes you do a reading because you've tried everything else and none of it has helped. So here you are . . . at the end of your rope.

This spread is designed for those times. It begins with a representation of yourself and the problem, then suggests something you can do to improve your situation, two possible sources of assistance, and a resting place where you can recharge. By the time you've climbed to the top of it, you won't be at the end of your rope anymore.

Choosing a Deck
The deck you use for a reading can influence the effectiveness. Some diviners keep only a single deck for all purposes. In that case, a nice balanced deck like the *Connolly Tarot* (my preferred teaching deck) is a good choice. Many diviners collect decks of different styles, though. It often helps to match the deck to the theme of the reading or the concept of the spread. This spread lends itself to positive decks, and is better read with all cards upright.

For example, the "End of Your Rope" spread works especially well with mystical decks, such as the *Vision Quest Tarot* by Gayan S. Winter and Jo Dosé. These cards feature Native American imagery, drawn from several tribes, to explore spiritual truths. Its relatively gentle touch helps resolve difficulties relating to the Earth and to divinity.

For really dire situations, consider the *Lord of the Rings Tarot* by Terry Donaldson, Peter Pracownik, and Mike Fitzgerald. This deck uses symbolism based on the writing of J.R.R. Tolkien. The artwork is regal, and the interpretations faithful to Tolkien's work. When you want the unvarnished truth, these cards will provide it.

The "End of Your Rope" spread also works well with non-tarot divinatory decks. The *Awareness Cards* by Susan Halliday present colorful images based on ancient art, such as petroglyphs and cave paintings. They are primal, powerful, and less language-oriented than many decks. Consider this deck for issues relating to past lives or the subconscious mind.

Laying the Spread

First, decide what to ask the cards. You need a clear idea of what is wrong, and a concise way to phrase it. Keep your question in mind as you shuffle the cards.

Lay out six cards. Put down the first card vertically, the second card horizontally across the first, then four more vertically forming a line above the first card. The spread should look like a rope with a knot at the bottom. Read from the bottom upward.

Card 1: Significator. Who you are now. This card identifies the role you play in the current situation. It may reveal new aspects, previously hidden, that give you a better grasp of what is happening and thus how to respond effectively. Or it may simply frame the obvious, which at least confirms that the reading is on track.

Card 2: Problem. What has you all tied up in knots. Here is the essence of the challenge you currently face. Pay careful attention to the limitations of the problem as expressed in this card. If it comes from the Minor Arcana, the matter is less serious and more susceptible to change than might otherwise seem the case. If this card comes from the Major Arcana, however, it indicates a situation firmly established in reality and based in more profound metaphysical patterns, hence more difficult to alter.

Card 3: Next Step. What you can do to climb out. Even very complex and obstinate problems can be tackled by pulling them into small, manageable bits. So this card suggests something that you can do, right now, to start improving your situation. It may seem trivial, or even tangential, to your main issue. Try it anyway.

Card 4: Hand of Flesh. A person who can help you. Here you may

find a hint toward a particular individual, or a profession, or even just a broad category of help. This covers all manner of practical assistance from other people in your life. Remember that you are not alone, and it's okay to ask for support. Often people would like to offer assistance, but they don't want to seem pushy, so they wait to be asked.

Card 5: Hand of Spirit. A higher power offering guidance. For some people this may mean a patron deity, for others an ancestral spirit or totem, or some other type of guide. When you run out of personal energy and you can't find your way anymore, spirituality can help you find your second wind.

Card 6: Ledge. A safe haven that you can reach. In all difficult journeys, it is important to find opportunities for rest and recovery. This card may direct you to a physical location, if its imagery reminds you of somewhere particular. It can also point to a particular state of mind, a virtue or ideal, or some other abstraction that can provide a similar sense of refuge. Whatever form it takes, this is a sanctuary where you can pause before resuming your struggle. It will always be achievable—but not necessarily within *easy* reach.

Interpretations

The "End of Your Rope" spread is open to different interpretations. The most obvious is to read the card meanings in order from the bottom of the spread to the top. However, you can gain more insight by also looking at the suits and at cards in relation to each other.

The suits reveal the theme of the reading, usually tying into the first (significator) or second (problem) cards, or sometimes both together. Swords suggest conflict based on foolishness, dishonor, or lack of discernment. Wands deal with stunted growth and the loss of creativity or passion. Cups concern relationship troubles and a disconnection from your intuition. Pentacles stand for issues of physical health, financial troubles, stagnation, or instability. Court Cards mean that the situation has especially strong "people" issues, rather than impersonal challenges. While the Minor Arcana concern everyday matters readily subject to change, the Major Arcana indicate powerful forces at play—not easily altered.

Next, consider the cards in pairs. Card One and Card Two go together, describing your interface with the problem. Card Three actually matches Card Six, explaining how to reach a better place. Card Four and Card Five work as a team: your allies in the material and spiritual realms.

Dorothy Kelly's book *Tarot Card Combinations* (Weiser Books, 2003) specializes in interpreting cards together. For example, the Two of Cups and Death as a pair indicate the end of a committed relationship, such as might appear at the beginning of the spread. Moving along, the progressive pair could reveal something like the Two of Pentacles and the Ten of Pentacles, suggesting a change of residence. The two helper cards tend to support each other—for instance, the Knight of Cups (flesh) and the King of Swords (spirit) point to a leadership opportunity. It is also worthwhile to compare the first and last cards in a reading.

In most spreads, reversals are an asset. For the "End of Your Rope," they are likely to be overkill: you're already stressed or you wouldn't be choosing this spread. So a deck that doesn't use reversals is usually a better choice here. Use your judgment and self-knowledge, though; if you prefer blunt truths, you might be more satisfied including them.

The "End of Your Rope" spread offers you a new way to approach a situation that has left you frustrated. It suggests things you can do to improve matters, while also acknowledging your need for support. The decisions you make are ultimately up to you—but at least you won't be swinging in the wind anymore.

Three-Card Readings

A Touch of Astrology

by Sally Cragin

I can't remember exactly how it happened, but some years back I had the opportunity to do some appearances at area bookstores to promote my *Moon Signs* calendar, and I ended up doing tarot readings. Hitherto, I had only done the occasional reading for myself, or for a friend whom I knew really well (it is *very* easy to do tarot readings for people whose biographies are familiar).

Serendipity and happenstance, I've found, are extremely useful factors when launching a new business, and when the store manager asked if I'd be willing to do tarot readings at $20 apiece, I said "Sure, why not." A twenty-minute reading for $20 seemed about right, but I definitely needed to find a useful card layout that wasn't quite as elaborate as the Celtic Cross (which uses ten to eleven cards, depending on your method).

If one has unlimited time to scrutinize a pile of cards, and really look at the imagery and what each picture might mean *and* what each picture means juxtaposed next to another, well, that's one thing. But twenty minutes is not very long at all. My astrological readings run seventy-five minutes, and that's an interval that flies by.

So I thought, "How simple can I make this, and also include some astrological information?" If I asked the clients their day/ month/year of birth, I could bring my ephemeris and look up Sun and Moon signs. If people knew their ascendants, so much the better, but even if they didn't, I have a chart that provides an "at a glance" rising sign, depending on sign. Yes, it is time for me to get a laptop computer with broadband access; still, I'm an old-fashioned astrologer who enjoys working out the geometry. I like to ask myself: What would John Dee (Queen Elizabeth I's astrologer) have done? What would Evangeline Adams have done?

To return to the tarot reading, the simplest scenario to construct is: past, present, future. I could have had the clients go through the deck and pick cards that "speak" to them, but I didn't want them to feel the time-pressure. So I just had them shuffle and cut the cards.

Some Information to Keep in Mind

Tarot and astrology have some useful elemental connections, and if you remember nothing else, remember that fire (Aries, Leo, Sagittarius), earth (Taurus, Virgo, Capricorn), air (Gemini, Libra, Aquarius) and water (Cancer, Scorpio, Pisces) translate to Wands, Pentacles, Swords, and Cups.

Sample Reading for Client Born April 3, 1971 (time not known)

Sun in Aries, Moon in Cancer (I'm sparing you the rest of the chart, since I'm planning to focus on these major planetary placements).

This Aries girl has her Moon square to her Sun (90 degrees away), so she's always got some tension between what she feels (deeply, truly) and what her Sun sign tells her in terms of how she "should" be. So just going in, any imagery with fire or water on the cards will be helpful because it helps explain "her."

The first card is the middle card: the here and now. She got the Knight of Pentacles. Since Pentacles is an earth sign, and I think of the Knight as having the number eleven (following the standard playing-card tradition of numbering), some questions might be: Do you know someone born on or around May, September, or January 11? Is that date significant in any way? If the answer is yes, then we know the reading may be about that person's connection with our client. And September 11 still affects many of us, even if we were nowhere near New York or Washington. If the answer is no, see if describing an earth-sign male (or earth-sign tomboy) rings any bells. Perhaps this is an aspect of our client's personality—a knight who goes off to battle armed with funds rather than weaponry. Is debt, or preoccupation with debt, a line of inquiry to pursue?

If so, let the client talk about how the card connects to her life and present circumstances. If she starts talking about the past—

which is inevitable, since we are constantly processing and evaluating past events to understand where we are and where we might be going—it's time for the next card.

The Past

This card is laid to the left of the first card you drew. As an example, we've drawn the Nine of Cups. This is a classic card representing material happiness; however, it does depict a person who could be interpreted as being, shall we say, a touch miserly? The person on this card is not really sharing those cups, and the folded arms represent a certain amount of smugness. So—the first question is to describe the card as I have done and ask, "Is there a Cancer, Scorpio, or Pisces in your life who could be represented here?"

Now, remember that our client has a Cancer Moon, so another question might be: "Does your satisfaction with material goods get in the way of having feelings or interaction with others?" Cancer Moon folks are always much more sensitive than the world thinks they are, and also more driven by an ideal of domestic happiness or sensual bliss. If our client says that "all the cups are empty," the cards are telling us that there may be too much solitude in this person's past (that, or misplaced generosity). Now remember, our client is an Aries, and Aries signs can get bored quickly, or need to leap from project to project. Is there a feeling of "groundedness" that our Aries client is rebelling against? Time for our final card.

The Future

This goes on the right side of the first card, so we now have a three-card sequence. This card can represent either personalities or projects unfolding, or how our Aries client might handle upcoming events. This card is the Four of Swords, reversed. The description of this is the effigy of a knight in the attitude of prayer, lying full length on his own tomb. The definition is fairly obvious—staying vigilant yet prayerful is suggested. This can be interpreted as the hermit's repose as well as a pause in current events. When the card is reversed, it doesn't lose much in its definition, but can take on monetary interpretation: economy, circumspection—in general, "wait and see," but only after taking a time-out.

Since Swords represent air signs (Gemini, Libra, or Aquarius), you might ask your client if there is anyone in her life currently with that birthday who can either encourage this behavior or who embodies this sort of repose. Contrary to popular belief, not all air signs are flighty stimulation junkies! Another way of having your client talk about the potential of this card is to ask if there is anything in her life that needs to be "cut away." While this knight is resting, his weapons are at the ready, with plenty for friends if need be.

Final Thoughts

Depending on how satisfactorily your three-card reading turns out, you may or may not want to put a fourth card down—a card to follow the immediate future. There are different spots for this interpretation on the classic Celtic Cross layout, and it is up to you, the card reader, to decide if a fourth card is needed. Sometimes the astrological elements of a reading don't seem to be ringing any bells for your client—or she's not aware of when people were born, so she doesn't know their signs. If that is the case, use the suit cards to describe personality traits that do go along with the elements. For example, Wands represent a fire-sign person or someone who can make executive decisions, loves to work, and brings a measure of excitement. Pentacles represent earth signs, and could suggest someone who's practical, wedded to routine, slow to respond. Swords are air signs, and could be someone who can't stay grounded; Cups are water signs, or people who are notably emotional and extremely susceptible to feeling.

Major Arcana: Arcane? Not Necessarily

I deliberately did a reading that used no Major Arcana and my advice to anyone learning how to read tarot is to separate the deck. Put

1 - The Magician

The Magician from The Celtic Dragon Tarot

the twenty-two Major Arcana cards in one pile. Put them in order, and then lay them out and tell a literal story. The Fool meets/becomes a Magician, meets/becomes a High Priestess, meets/becomes the Empress, and so on. It's pretty likely that you'll get at least one member of the Major Arcana in a three-card reading—to get two ups your significance, and to get three means, well, how carefully *did* you shuffle that deck?

Actually, the first couple of times the Strength card and Moon card turned up in readings, the more inclined was I to ask, "Who's the Leo in your life?" and "Who's the Cancer?" Both of those cards depict unequivocal astrological imagery. Lions are Leo, and the Moon rules Cancer.

The Major Arcana accelerate the narrative aspects of a reading, and some cards have obvious astrological resonance. The Emperor's ram imagery evokes Aries; Justice, with its scales and sword (air), is Libra to a T; and the World, with eagle (Aries), bull (Taurus), and lion (Leo) could be an event that carries from spring through summer.

Some cards put me in mind of certain personality traits or seem to connect with each other. I can't see the Fool without mentally filling in the next card, its opposite in characteristics, the Magician. What the Fool doesn't know, the Magician is always planning. The next group is a quartet: High Priestess, Empress, Emperor, and Hierophant. The figures having religious/spiritual weight bookend the two figures signifying worldly success and authority. Could these be direct, confident cardinal-sign folks (Aries, Cancer, Libra, Capricorn) or those who fill that space in the client's life?

The next group I think of as a collective are VI to XV, which begins with the Lovers and ends with the Lovers enthralled to the Devil. The story you can tell using the Chariot, Strength, the Hermit, Wheel of Fortune, Justice, the Hanged Man, Death, Temperance, and the Devil presents a seemingly paradoxical collection: passion followed by indifference or its opposition. Most people get very nervous when that Death or Devil card shows up, but for me, the deal-breaker is the Tower.

How to interpret? The will to self-destruction is strong in our species, and this is where you ask your client if there's anything really bothering her that this card brings to mind. The fire imagery (Aries, Leo, Sagittarius) is pretty apparent, and in the wake of September 11, we can put a dire interpretation on that card. But remember—it also represents the Tower of Babel, and since talking is an air-sign activity, this card could prompt a discussion about someone who talks too much or says too much or isn't always understood. Perhaps this is your client?

The remaining cards, Star, Moon, Sun, Judgement, and World, are definitely concluding cards, and if one of them is the third (or fourth card) in the reading, a satisfactory outcome to the problem that emerged from the reading is more likely. Those are happy-looking cards also, and people are generally delighted to see them.

The more you do three-card readings, the more you'll find that your mind and mouth will begin to edit the necessarily limited narrative that emerges with just three storyboards. The most important lesson to learn from reading cards for others is the importance of listening. Let the cards talk and the client talk. And then you can talk.

The Hermit

For Further Study

L'EREMITA
L'ERMITE
IX
THE HERMIT
EL ERMITAÑO

DER EREMIT
DE KLUIZENAAR

The Answer Is in the Question

by James Wells

One of the ways I describe my tarot practice is "inquiry-based." It means that a good tarot consultation is rooted and grounded in well-phrased, open-ended questions and in interpreting any cards that turn up in light of those questions. Whether in session with clients or teaching groups of students, I rarely use prefabricated tarot layouts such as the Celtic Cross or Tree of Life spreads. Instead, I prefer to design a spread that is appropriate to the person's topic of inquiry in that moment. This layout is based entirely upon the querent's questions and any other questions that I might suggest to round things out. This allows the client to receive more specific and useful feedback from his or her source of wisdom via the cards. It also keeps me on track, ensuring that I don't wander onto irrelevant informational trails.

My beginners' class and many of my advanced classes and workshops include segments on the art of helpful or constructive questions and how to turn these questions into a layout. I am amazed afresh every time a tarot consultant/reader spends time identifying a topic, creates questions around that topic, turns these questions into a layout, and lays out the cards only to interpret the pasteboards before him or her in a manner that has nothing whatsoever to do with the spread position, question, or area of inquiry.

A couple of examples may illustrate this. In one tarot class, a young woman asked, "What obstacle could potentially block this endeavor?" and drew the Sun card from her face-down tarot pack. Her immediate response to receiving this card was, "Oh look . . . the Sun card . . . there aren't any blocks . . . everything is just fine." A thirty-something man in another workshop asked, "What is my greatest strength in this situation?" and got the Ten of Swords. He was beside himself and exclaimed, "I don't have any strengths!" In both cases, the readers got so caught up in the card and what they thought it "should" mean that they entirely forgot to relate it to their questions.

In the way that I work with tarot, the card you get *is* the answer. It is a direct response to the question that is posed. Why else would it turn up? The topic agreed upon by both reader and querent and its consequent layout are a contract between reader, querent, and the universe. It's an agreement on what we are here to explore today, at this time. Not something else, but *this*. If a CEO told her board members that a meeting would be called to discuss the budget, she would not use the time to plan the office holiday party. If Sue asks Bob, "What time is it?" she probably wants to hear something like, "It's half-past two." It's not terribly helpful to Sue if Bob comes back with, "I'll have an order of fries and a milkshake."

A tarot consultation is a conversation. Constructive, interesting conversations occur when both parties listen to what is asked, and then respond as fully as possible to those questions. If someone comes for a tarot consultation and the topic is about increasing his or her financial income over the next six months, I don't start talking about the cards in light of romance. If my client wants to explore the next stage in his or her personal growth, I don't prattle on about alien soulmates from Atlantis (not that I would do this anyway!).

Let's revisit the two people in the third paragraph to illustrate this point that the answer is in the question. The young woman in my class who got the Sun about potential blocks could have interpreted it as a need to be the "center of the solar system," rebirthing old habits in a new disguise, or acting childishly.

The Fool from *Ship of Fools Tarot*

0 THE VAGABOND

The fellow whose Ten of Swords answered, "What is my greatest strength?" could have discovered these particular gifts in himself: an ability to hold back from speaking too soon, avoidance of idle chat or gossip, and a willingness to take time out from his regular schedule in order to regenerate himself.

All of this illustrates my basic mantra or formula for creating meaning: topic + question (or spread position) + card = meaning.

Activities

A. Sort your face-up tarot cards into two piles: positive/constructive and negative/challenging. Select a few cards from your positive stack and come up with negative interpretations for each. Perhaps "creative" becomes "devious," or "courageous" turns into "foolhardy." Now pick cards from your negative pile and find positive slants for each. "Delusion" could become "imagination," and "stagnation" might be seen as "stillness." My point here is that cards and their core meanings are essentially neutral. Our questions will tilt their interpretations one way or the other.

B. Explore the power of open-ended questions. Write them in your journal, speak them in groups, read them in books on communication processes. Employ questions that begin with "how," "what," or "where in my life." "Why" questions can be okay as long as they don't encourage victimization (e.g., "Why always me?"). And practice asking questions that refer to yourself or your role in something. This sets a tone of personal responsibility.

If someone comes to me for a consultation and asks, "Should I quit my job?" I would invite him or her to go further, to ask open-ended questions such as:

* What do I enjoy most about my current work environment?

* What about my current work environment do I find most challenging?

* Which of my needs are being met in this current job?

* Which of my needs are not being met in this current job?

* What skills am I able to utilize in this job?

* What skills am I not able to utilize in this job?

* How do I contribute to the situation at work?

* How might I contribute to the solution for the situation at work?

We would then pull a card (or more than one card) to respond to each question.

C. Select a topic for which you'd like to do a tarot reading. Choose or create an appropriate layout. On a big sheet of paper, draw a diagram of this layout with card-sized spread positions. Label each position so you remember clearly what each one is about. Mix your deck. Select one card from the pack and write down its name. Place this card on the first layout position, and interpret it according to that position's intent. Remove the card from the first position and place it on the second one. Now interpret the card in light of this position. Continue to do this until your single card has visited every part of the spread. You'll notice how the card's meaning shifts according to where it is in the layout.

For example, I was curious about the ideas in this article, so I designed a three-card layout:

1. What's the best thing people can do with regard to using questions in their tarot practice?

2. What's the worst thing people can do with regard to using questions in their tarot practice?

3. How might this article change people's tarot practice for the better?

From the *Shining Tribe* tarot deck, I get the Nine of Stones. When I place it on the "best thing" position, I'm drawn to the stars that have been brought down into the stones. So the Nine of Stones suggests that we bring lofty concepts down to earth, that we ground life's big questions in reality, that questions based on what we know in real life will show us the mysteries of the cosmos. In the "worst thing" position, I notice that the central figure is alone in her stone garden with her face turned away from the light. So the same card suggests that it's not good for us to try and ask these questions alone. Perhaps fellow tarot practitioners can be of value to us on our quest for helpful questions. On the figure's shoulder is a hooded falcon which gives me the message that it's not a good idea to cover up our instinct to hunt for deeper answers or to ask richer questions. In the third position, the Nine of Stones says that by applying the ideas and activities in this article to your tarot practice, you can create a personal "garden" or secure haven in which you feel safe enough to explore your instinctive questions. You'll have an ongoing structure to keep you on track and give the light of truth tangible form in the world. May it be so!

Pathworking

by Magenta Griffith

Pathworkings are a type of guided meditation based on the Major Arcana of the tarot. The idea of guided meditation for spiritual purposes goes back to St. Ignatius of Loyola in the sixteenth century, if not earlier. These exercises are based on the Tree of Life diagram, and derive from the Kabbalah, a school of Jewish mysticism dating back at least to the thirteenth century. Such meditations were performed by the Order of the Golden Dawn, and many of the versions in use today derive from Golden Dawn materials. Usually, these are located indoors in artificial settings, such as formal temples, and involve angelic forms as messengers and guides. As a Pagan, I found it difficult to relate to some of these images, so I composed my own. The Pathworkings of Nature use settings such as woods, deserts, caves, and waterfalls to evoke the principles of the cards.

The Tree of Life maps several symbol systems onto one representation. Tarot, numerology, and astrology are all interrelated by this system. The diagram consists of ten circles, representing the spheres, and twenty-two lines, the paths between them. The spheres correspond to the numbers one through ten, and therefore to both the tarot cards Ace through Ten and the numbers one through ten for numerology. The twenty-two paths correspond

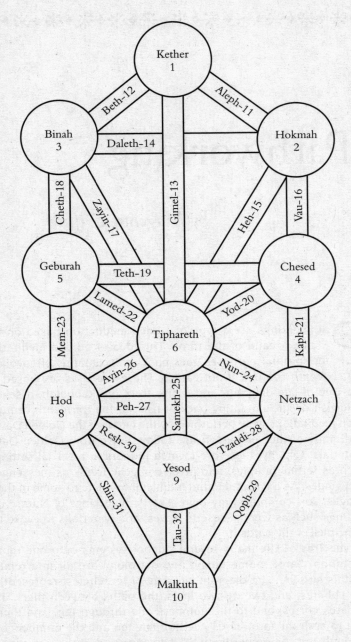

The Paths of the Tree of Life

to the Major Arcana of the tarot deck, but are numbered eleven through thirty-two, because the numbers one through ten already represent the ten spheres.

To people who study Kabbalah, this is not just a diagram, but a map of the world. Only the lowest sphere represents physical reality; the rest are levels of existence on non-physical planes, with the uppermost sphere representing the Godhead.

The lowest sphere is called Malkuth, "Kingdom," and corresponds to the physical world. The path from Malkuth to the next sphere, Yesod, "Foundation," is path number Thirty-Two and is represented by the World card. Yesod is the lowest astral plane, so this is the path from the physical to the astral. Almost everyone travels this path, often without realizing it: in dreams, during illness, even when daydreaming. The purpose of this pathworking is to follow it deliberately, to come to Yesod consciously.

Preparing for a Pathworking

Successful pathworkings require some preparation. You may wish to follow a specific script, at least for the first few times. After that, it is possible to study the card of the path you wish to work, immerse yourself in its symbolism, and use that as a starting point for your meditation.

If you wish to use a written pathworking, and you work alone, you will either have to record your own tapes or split your attention enough to read the pathworking and visualize the path at the same time. The latter may take some practice. If you work with others, people can take turns reading the pathworking, or record it in advance so that all may participate. In either case, read the material several times in advance.

First, you will want to have a quiet place where you will be undisturbed. Interruptions are seldom dangerous, contrary to what you might find in occult fiction. However, it can be difficult to relax knowing you can easily be interrupted. Unplug the phone. Put a sign on your door: "Meditating, Please Do Not Disturb."

You will need to sit or lie comfortably. An easy chair is one solution, a mat on the floor is another. Some people find they will fall asleep if they are lying down, while others find it easier to fall into trance when horizontal. If you do have a tendency to sleep but have no other place to work than your bed, try propping yourself up with extra pillows.

Get comfortable in all ways possible. Use the bathroom. Have water handy, especially for anyone who will be reading aloud or otherwise talking in the course of the working. Wear comfortable, loose-fitting clothes, or magical robes. Take off your shoes. Most importantly, put aside all worries and mental distractions. Some people find it useful to have writing materials handy, both for recording their experiences and for listing things they are thinking about beforehand so they can let go of those thoughts.

It is best to do this sort of work at least an hour after a meal, because a full stomach may encourage sleep, and tends to discourage astral vision. On the other hand, being hungry can be a distraction as well. Plan to have a snack available after you are done; it will help ground you.

You will need a tarot deck, and the tree of life diagram would be useful. Put the card for the path you are working, in this case the World card, on your altar or wherever it will be visible during the working. Choose the card from your favorite deck, the one you use the most and feel most comfortable with.

What follows is an example of a pathworking. The first part, the temple of Malkuth, is a clearing in the woods. I have used this image repeatedly, and it has been much the same every time. What happens after entering the cave and walking the paths varies, both because of differences in the paths, and differences in the people doing the pathworking. Your experience of the path, and of the sphere of Yesod, may vary from this description. Go with what feels right to you.

The Working of Path Thirty-Two, Malkuth to Yesod

If you wish, cast a circle in your usual manner. Get into a relaxed position, either lying down or sitting with some back support. Visualize the following scene it as if you were there. Release from your mind the idea of "real" and "unreal." Imagine all that follows as vividly as you can.

You are in a clearing in a wooded area. To the south is a fire burning in a firepit. To the west is a brook, gushing over rocks. To the east, the land drops off sharply, and you gaze out at clouds floating in the distance and birds flying through the blue sky. To the north, the land rises up steeply, and there is the mouth of a cave.

In the center of clearing is a low stone altar. On the altar is a simple pottery cup or chalice and a stone knife, perhaps of some pale flint. There are wax spots on the altar, where candles have burned down. The altar itself is perhaps a foot high, of stone roughly shaped. It is about three feet wide and two feet across. There is also a pentacle of bronze or other dull metal, and a porcelain incense burner, for burning resin on coals.

The fire burns high: you can see the flames leap, hear the wood crackle, smell the smoke. You can also hear the stream gurgling and splashing from time to time. The area on the other side of the stream is wooded. Sometimes when you look east you see birds, or hear them call. It is always quiet to the north.

The land slopes gently down at the south, and very slightly at the west. The stream flows north to south, of course, and the land slopes that way as well.

You move to the mouth of the cave. You find that it is a little taller than you are, and you can enter without ducking your head. The light is dim inside, but you can still see what is around you. There are three passages inside the cave: one to the left, one to the right, and one that goes straight ahead. You begin walking down the middle passage, the path that goes straight back from the mouth of the cave.

The rock is hard and uneven under your feet, the rough walls of grey stone curve above you. There is enough space below the ceiling not to feel cramped. It is dark, but you can see light up ahead, and you move toward it. Gradually, you notice the walls less and less, and the passage seems to widen until it feels like you are no longer walking through rock. The rock has changed into tall trees and dense underbrush. You keep walking and finally find yourself in the open.

You are standing at the edge of a large grassy field. There are many people here, or perhaps "beings" is a better word. There are also animals, and mythological beings like fauns, gargoyles, and elves. The weather is pleasant—bright and sunny. A few large trees shade the area.

The beings are dancing, though the exact pattern is unclear because you can't see the whole dance. There are only a few around the edge of the field, but as you get farther in, more and more are moving around. You may move or dance with them, staying at the edge of the group or moving toward the center. You may find yourself near enough to the center to see if there is a central figure, such as a large goddess statue, or even the Goddess herself, dancing. You may

◆　interact with the various beings who are dancing, or with the central
✳︎　figure. There is a clockwise motion to the group of people moving and
◆　dancing. Whether you stay at the periphery or farther in, gradually
　move with them, clockwise, around to the "other side" of the circle.

When you have reached the far side of the circle of people, start walking away from the group. Eventually, you will find yourself in a tunnel through rock again. Ahead is a doorway. There may be a door, or a curtain over a doorway, with a picture of a crescent moon, or the number nine. There may be other symbols on the door as well, perhaps one or all of the Nines from your tarot cards. Go through the curtain or open the door and go in.

This is the sphere of Yesod, Foundation. This is the start of the astral planes. In here, it may seem misty, hazy, smoky. The light is dim, colored violet or purple. You may hear faint music. The place will seem very large, perhaps with dimly perceived forms; you can't tell if there are other people there or not. There is a central altar that is a nine-sided stone. If you decide to approach it, you may see it is made of amethyst. Notice whether there are any objects on the altar. When you are ready to leave, turn and exit through the door you entered. It will have the number thirty-two on or over it, or there will be a picture of the card on the door.

You will find yourself in another tunnel through rock. You walk back, and after a while find a step going up. You step up, and know you are halfway back to Malkuth. Keep walking, and you soon emerge from the cave. Spend a moment or two in the clearing, then feel yourself back in the room where you started, and open your eyes.

Take a few minutes to think about what you have experienced. Write it down, if you like. Then end your circle, if you cast one, or otherwise end the ritual. Have something to eat and drink, either in circle or immediately afterward.

Tarot and Death

Part One

by Nina Lee Braden

I've been especially interested in the Death card from very early in my tarot studies. I'm a Scorpio, and Scorpio is commonly associated with the Death card. Rather than becoming alarmed or upset about this association, I took the challenge to enthusiastically seek out the special message of this card for me.

In my tarot studies, I learned that the Death card did not signal death, did not predict death, and that ethical tarotists did not predict death for their clients when the Death card came up. Instead, I was trained to think of the meaning of the Death card as transformation, transition, and rebirth. When the Death card comes up in a reading, it doesn't mean that the querent or someone close to the querent will die. If it did, the world population would be much smaller. Therefore, to suggest that someone will die whenever the Death card comes up would be irresponsible. We need to look at other meanings of the Death card for our readings. Additionally, cards other than the Death card can suggest death, so the absence of the Death card may not mean an absence of deaths or transformations. In other words, Death is not just death, and death is not just in the Death card.

Historically, however, the figure on the Death card is the angel of death himself. After all, during the time of the earliest recorded tarot cards, death was very common. The Black Plague was rampant throughout Europe. Mortality rates were high. Wood-block prints and stained-glass windows frequently pictured the figure of Death walking along the road, entering a home, or conversing with the average citizen. Death as the end of life, and death as an allegorical figure, were both well known to the average person. Early viewers of the Death card would have definitely thought of death rather than rebirth or transformation.

But we live in the twenty-first century, not the late Middle Ages. Although the history of the tarot and its historical meanings will always be important, tarot today is not the same as it was hundreds of years ago, and the way that we see and view the cards has naturally evolved over the centuries.

In tarot today, the Death card is still one of the most feared and most often misunderstood cards. Death is the card that suggests change, renewal, destruction (but not sudden or radical destruction), and rebirth. It is winter going into spring. It is eliminating the old and going on to the new. It is transformation, regeneration. It is the caterpillar turning into the butterfly. Humans fear change, and we often fear the changes indicated by the Death card.

Death Mandalas

Make a list of your favorite meanings for the Death card. Some of them might include change, transformation, purification, journeys,

13 DEATH

Death from *Ship of Fools Tarot*

sleep, sex, and rebirth. Next, go through your tarot deck face-up and set aside each card that also has one of those meanings. For example, if I were thinking about Death as travel, I would put aside the Six of Swords, the Eight of Cups, the Chariot, the four Knights, the Fool, the Moon, the Hermit, the Wheel of Fortune, the Ten of Wands, the Three of Wands, the Six of Wands, the Seven of Swords, and the Eight of Wands. Your choices will vary, and my choices would also vary somewhat on a different day or with a different deck. Arrange all of the cards in a circle, and put the Death card in the center. What insights can you get from studying the "Travel Mandala" of Death?

Similarly, you can choose the meaning of Death as "transformation." What other cards mean or suggest transformation? The Tower, Judgement, Temperance, the Hanged Man, the four Aces, the Empress, and the Ten of Swords might be a few. You would then create a "Transformation Mandala" of Death using these cards in a circle and the Death card in the center.

Death and Scorpio

There are many different systems that pair tarot cards and the signs of the zodiac. My favorite system pairs the Death card with the sign of Scorpio. Scorpio has several different animals associated with it. The eagle represents the higher level of Scorpio, the snake the mid-level (which can serve either good or evil), and the scorpion the lower level of Scorpio. The Death card can reveal a higher nature, like the eagle soaring high above. Like the snake, it can show a mixed situation, with many sides in conflict. Like the scorpion, it can allude to the basest nature of humans. Sometimes Scorpio is also seen as the phoenix, the mythical bird that dies in a glorious burst of flames and then rises again from its ashes. Certainly, the phoenix has an obvious association with the Death card.

With the pairing of Death and Scorpio, we also get an association between the Death card and Samhain or All Hallow's Eve. Samhain is celebrated roughly halfway between the Fall Equinox and Winter Solstice. To Pagans and Christians, Samhain's principle function is as a memorial day. To Pagans, it is the day to say farewell to all those who have crossed over during the previous year. To Christians, All Hallow's Day (also called All Saint's Day) is a day to remember Christian saints and martyrs. Many Hispanics celebrate this time as the Day of the Dead. The day can also be about grieving in general and remembering those who have passed in previous years, not just the current year. A related theme of Samhain is releasing negative emotions, destructive habits, and unhealthy thought patterns. After all, the Death card is about rebirth. When one thing dies, something else is born.

Samhain is also the third and final harvest. In agricultural societies, it is an actual harvest. For us, the harvest may be more symbolic. Again, the Death card applies. One message of the Death card is that as we sow, so shall we reap. The figure on the Death card frequently carries a scythe to harvest souls as it makes its journey.

♦   And for those of us in the northern hemisphere, the shortening
☀ days at Samhain are a signal that we are going into the repair/regen-
♦ eration/rest portion of the year, and of course repair, regeneration,
and rest are meanings for the Death card. It is very easy to use the
Death card as a part of a seasonal observance.

Other Death Correspondences

Not only are there correspondences between tarot and astrology,
but there are numerous other correspondences: colors, musical
notes, Hebrew letters, herbs, and more. Some of these correspondences may resonate for you and some may not, but it's frequently
quite fruitful to choose one or two correspondences from a list and
meditate on them in connection with the Death card. For example,
the musical note associated with the Death card is G. If you are
a musician, this may have meaning for you. Even if you are not
a musician, a little further study may make that correspondence
tell you something. There are more Major Arcana cards than there
are notes in a scale, so some cards share notes—but no other card
shares G. So, musically, Death stands alone. Two cards, the Empress
and Justice, share F-sharp, the note immediately before G. So, musically, the Empress and Justice come before Death. Three cards, the
High Priestess, the Hanged Man, and Temperance, share G-sharp,
the note immediately after G. So, musically, the High Priestess, the
Hanged Man, and Temperance follow Death. What thoughts do
these correspondences suggest to you? There are no right or wrong
answers, only gateways to new discoveries. You can follow similar
procedures with other sets of correspondences.

Tarot Math and Death

One way to think of the Death card is numerically, as the number
thirteen. Thirteen is a prime number, which means that it is only
divisible by itself and one. However, some esotericists like to play
around with a form of tarot math or tarot numerology: they look at
each card in a variety of ways in order to gain deeper insights to the
card. For example, we can contemplate thirteen as the sum of one
and twelve. We can then think of how the Magician (card I) plus
the Hanged Man (card XII) give us additional insight into the Death
card. For example, if I hang upside down and allow myself to be a
channel for divine energy, do I become the pope in the Death card?
Or am I the purified desire of the white flower on Death's flag?

   In similar fashion, we can look at the High Priestess (II) and
Justice (XI) and so on for what they tell us about the Death card. We

can even use three or more cards, looking at the Empress (III) plus the Emperor (IV) plus the Lovers (VI) for how all three cards work together to tell us something about the Death card.

Death from *The Universal Tarot*

Discovering Death Exercise

One of the meanings of the Death card is transformation. There are many kinds of transformation and many degrees of transformation. Every twenty-four hours, night is transformed into day, which is transformed back into night. In a lifetime, we transform from infancy to childhood to adolescence to adulthood to maturity to old age, unless we die before completing the life cycle. If we expand our awareness of transformation more broadly, we can look at evolution as transformation. Animal life began simply, probably in the ocean. One day, a water creature developed lungs instead of gills. Later, a lung-breather crawled up on land and became a forerunner of what would evolve into the human race.

Think of a general transformation, not a transformation that is unique to your life. This transformation could be the twenty-four hour cycle, the year cycle (if you live where there are distinct seasons), a species cycle (caterpillar to cocoon to butterfly), or an even broader cycle. Choose a cycle that you are familiar with, one that you know something about.

What cycle did you choose? What is the general timeline or development or unfolding of stages for this cycle?

Although the Death card is the one card that most strongly suggests transformation, other cards can also mean transformation. Using the deck of your choice, remove the Death card and any other cards that seem to have a message of transformation in them.

Using the cards that you have chosen, tell the story of your transformation cycle. You need not use all of the cards.

There have been many stories, poems, novels, plays, and movies that personify death, bring death to life (so to speak), and use death as a character who interacts with others. Emily Dickinson did it, Edgar Allan Poe did it, and Alberto Casella did it in *Death Takes a Holiday* (later remade as *Meet Joe Black*). You do the same. Pretend that death becomes human and comes to visit. What is death like? Is death male or female? What does death look like? Does death have a British accent? Look like Brad Pitt? Look like Medusa? Look like your grandmother? Look like a jackal-headed man? Look like an angel? How would you see death if death were to knock at your front door?

Although death is not the same as the Death card, there are certain and obvious connections. Have your personified death tell the story of your transformation cycle. How does the story differ when death tells it?

Put all of your cards back into your deck (or pull out a fresh deck). Shuffle your deck and deal cards for each of the following:

What is transformation?

Who or what is death?

How is the Death card like death?

How is the Death card unlike death?

How is the Death card like transformation?

How is the Death card unlike transformation?

What cards come up? How do you interpret the answers? Choose one area of your life that you would like to transform. What is it? Think of a concrete step that you can do today that would be an active step towards transformation. Do it.

Not the End

Although I've spent many years studying the Death card, I am constantly amazed at the new insights that the card provides. I love its mystery, power, and mysticism. I enjoy studying its various occult correspondences. I recognize its connection to death, but I love to explore the full extent of its meanings and symbols. I find it the most fascinating card in the deck. May I have many more years to explore the secrets of Death.

Turning Inward

by Ruth Ann and Wald Amberstone

T arot is a tool, an instrument. This is true for most tarot people most of the time. It was created to serve, and serve it has for several hundred years.

It has served long and well as a tool for divination, and for many that is its only function. For some, tarot serves as a mnemonic device for an elaborate system of ceremonial magic, and also as a ritual tool in the workings of that magic. Because that magic has philosophical and mystical implications, tarot acquired those same qualities and serves those purposes as well.

In recent times, psychology has been added to tarot's resume. Using tarot as a tool for psychological insight has been the leading edge of tarot theory for several decades now and it still dominates the attention of a large number of modern tarot thinkers. This dominance led to the wonderfully defining question, "Psychology saved tarot from esotericism. What will save tarot from psychology?" asked by Rachel Pollack at the 2006 Readers Studio.

In fact, tarot has been "saved" more than once and will be again. Divination saved tarot from the trivialities of play. Esotericism rescued tarot from the melodrama of early fortune-telling. Victorian scholarship saved tarot from the mythologies of eighteenth-century esotericism, and psychology has saved tarot once again from twentieth-century versions of nineteenth-century esoteric spirituality.

Each of these salvations has simultaneously moved tarot forward and left each preceding layer of development in place and essentially untouched. We think this is as it should be.

Each "salvation" has looked back on what preceded it with a combination of fondness, condescension, relief, and incomprehension, mixed in varying proportions according to individual taste.

Each has moved progressively inward over time. From the original competitiveness of play all the way through the modern insights of personal psychology, the flow of interest has moved like a great, lazy river in one general direction.

Like travelers on a river, our individual visions of tarot are limited to what lies between the bend behind us and the bend ahead. We experience the current as it is happening. We understand it only as it passes into history behind us. Of what is to come, we hear a little and see nothing.

But it is a cliché used by all modern readers that the future is ultimately ours to make out of what we have been given. In tarot, what we are given is our history, our experience, and our imagination.

We propose a perspective that combines all three ingredients and makes a vessel on which anyone who likes it can sail into their own future. It can be called "tarot turned inward."

There is an outward and an inward tarot, an outward and an inward vision. The outward vision is the perspective of small beings looking into an immense universe. From this perspective, tarot does its best to help us and to explain us to ourselves in the context of what is called reality. But in that reality everything is an object, including us—our physical selves and all our qualities, seen and unseen. Our thoughts, feelings, intentions, and activities are all objects seen in a mirror.

There is always a "we" looking at "us," a mysterious subject observing and experiencing a complicated object. In tarot, "we" look at, talk about, work with, and help our various selves in every manner and form we can think of. We do this equally in a reading, a ritual, a meditation, or a self-examination. Even when the object of our attention is as rarified as our soul, it is still an object, and tarot is still turned outward. This perspective is so self-evident and pervasive it seems inescapable. The natural question arises, "What else is there?"

We think there is something else. It has always been there. It is made of the same stuff and looks pretty much the same. That "something else" is tarot turned inward.

When tarot turns inward, it ceases to be a mirror in which objects are reflected. It isn't interested in helping or understanding anyone. It predicts nothing, expresses nothing, counsels no one. It does better than that.

What might that be? And how could it happen? It's a very high kind of magic and tarot is nothing but magic. We can start there, with a high kind of magic, a sleight of hand that reveals instead of deceives.

We can use tarot to slow and eventually stop the outward-turning vision that creates a world of objects. Then tarot turns our vision inward and begins to reassemble our selves and the world before our eyes. A transmutation occurs, and we experience alchemy.

This is worth doing. It takes a while, but we're trying to slow things down anyway, so there's no harm in that. The trick is to make a beginning, which we think we can do. Shall we?

Our beginning is in two familiar words—outward and inward—ordinary words when you use them in an ordinary way. But tarot isn't ordinary.

When we use tarot, it's always in an outward-turning direction. Even when tarot becomes psychological or spiritual, that doesn't change. It's still a tool, and tools turn us outward into the waking, knowing, doing world we think of as real.

"Tarot turned inward," though, is a phrase that doesn't refer to anything we know, and that's as it should be because it's intended to invoke the unknown.

We could say that reality is a world of answers made manifest, and that the unknown is the source of questions. Together, question and answer make the rhythm of tarot, like breathing in and breathing out.

When we come to tarot we come with questions—questions of two kinds. The first are questions whose answers are firmly rooted in what we know. The second are questions whose answers lie in the unknown. The first kind of question asks tarot to confirm us in our knowledge and give us the answers that make the world. The second kind carries us away from what we know, past the boundary markers of our ignorance. The first kind of question is easy to ask. The second kind is not so easy.

It is only in the unknown that the world and ourselves can be reassembled. It is only there that we can turn tarot inward. If that is what we want to do, there is where we need to begin. But in a known world that encompasses everything, where is the unknown to be found?

Sometimes, it jumps at us from out of nowhere in the form of something seen or heard or felt for which we have no ready explanation. We ask ourselves, "What does *that* mean?" Or, "What just happened?" and we find ourselves without an answer. This is the unknown in the form of mystery. People who can confront us with mystery at will are magicians, whether they call themselves that or not. Their function is to make us wonder, to make us question what we know, to expand our sense of the possible, even if only for a moment. Stage magicians, psychics, shamans, and the best of teachers all do this as their stock in trade.

Initiation and induction into traditions of special knowledge can also do this in a very powerful way. On one level, tarot is just such a tradition. Esoteric tarot can substantially and permanently change your perception of both the deck and the world by revealing what is hidden, little by little, so that you come to know more and more.

Most tarot people these days are well aware of this. Even if you don't have an extensive acquaintance with esoteric tarot, you know it's there and it is accessible to you if you want to learn it. Esotericism means a knowledge of and belief in the inner nature of a thing. But it can be, and mostly is, just the core, the fountainhead, of the outward-turning perspective that gives us tarot as we know it. Hidden knowledge doesn't reassemble tarot. It just adds to and deepens it.

But deep and hidden knowledge, valuable as it is, doesn't get us where we want to go. It doesn't even point the direction. Explanations, even deep ones, only expand the empire of the known.

The unknown that remains forever unexplained passes into the realm of the unknowable. It is from what is unknowable in us that a sense of mystery arises and by which that mystery is sustained. Mystery's legacy is a state of perpetual surprise, a state of wonder, freshness and challenge without end. If we are not mistaken, this is where tarot leads when it turns inward.

Once again we're confronted with the question, "Where do we find the unknown and forever unknowable?" What questions can we ask of tarot that would turn it in a direction where information, no matter how useful, is unimportant?

Questions of this kind arise from whatever in the questioner is alive, unfixed, and unfinished.

We could say, without fear of being wrong, that every action of everyone's life is in some way an answer to an implicit question. A person with no questions at all would probably find it hard to draw breath. It may well be that human life depends on its questions, which are its continuous connection to the unknown.

Tarot is an engine for generating questions and answering them. Every question arises from the unknown and either invokes the unknown from without or evokes it from within, turning the attention of the questioner either outward or inward.

Answering questions about our lives and situations turns us outward. This is what we habitually and almost exclusively do. But tarot can do something else, something unknown. It can speak as, rather than to, the questioner. It can speak with the voice of what is forever mysterious and unknowable within ourselves, the fountain of life that flows into us and becomes the stuff of which we are made.

To ask questions arising from this place in ourselves is to drink from the fountain. We do this instinctively without knowing that we do it. In a very deep way, it keeps us alive and gives us whatever potential we possess. To do this consciously is to have power over what we manifest and fill it with a fierce and irresistible joy. We can do this with tarot.

Whoever did this would do it in their own way. Such questions are as personal as signatures. But what would such a question be like? It might be very like things you've heard before, yet not at all the same. An ordinary question can be reframed to concern itself with a state of being instead of an outcome.

For example:

"When will I meet my soulmate?" might become "If I were somebody's soul mate, what would I be? Can I be someone's soulmate as I am?"

"Will I win my lawsuit?" might become "Will the outcome of my lawsuit change who or what I am, or what I might become?"

Here's a question someone asked us recently. It went like this: "My forties taught me painful lessons I needed to learn. My fiftieth birthday scared me because I had grown up thinking fifty is old, but I discovered my strength in my fifties. As I approached my sixtieth birthday, I wondered what my sixties would bring me. Now I want to know what I will take with me into my seventies."

Here is another much more extreme example. "I think I'm going insane. My insides are doing things I think they shouldn't. I'm a student of tantra in a serious way, have been for ten years. It's messy stuff, not what people think. It messes up your mind. But when you've gone this far, you can't really stop. It changes you and you can't go back. Am I turning into a monster or some kind of a freak? Will I be all right? What *is* all right, for me?"

Questions like these appeal to us, though they might or might not be questions you would ask or be able to answer. Their spirit seems to turn tarot inward and demand that tarot become the answer in order to speak. No satisfactory responses could come in the form of objective information, nor would they be about anything.

The answers would have to *be* something. Instead of knowing the answers, the questioners would have to become the answers. The fountain of the unknowable would flow through them in a continuous living experience. From this perspective, tarot is not *about* us. It *is* us.

We think it is possible not only to know but to become tarot, to possess it inside and out. With tarot turned outward, we can see what is visible, explore what is hidden and discover what is knowable. With tarot turned inward, we can navigate the unknown.

We are talking about tarot but we haven't mentioned a single card or technique or piece of knowledge. Without knowledge and technique, some concrete way to approach and manifest it, tarot turned inward remains just a possibility, an idea. Let's see if we can begin to make it real.

Earlier, we mentioned a sleight of hand, a magic trick that reveals instead of deceives. What if tarot were not made of suits and numbers and trumps and court cards, but of worlds and depths and paths and powers? What if the familiar names and images of tarot were really mysteries and secrets? It is the special magic of esotericism to accomplish this transformation of the ordinary into the extraordinary.

When you first open yourself to the teachings of esoteric tarot, you are confronted by a whole world you've never seen. Answers are given to questions you never thought to ask, and the cards acquire powers you never knew they had. Tarot becomes new without changing a thing. The only difference is in the eye of the beholder, in what you learn to see. The unknown is invoked, and a sense of wonder is induced. Both of these are essential to turning inward, so acquiring a knowledge of esoteric tarot is an essential first step. It can be a long step, and we can't tell you how to do it here, but it must be done.

Esoteric tarot can, and most often does, remain a matter of knowledge. It can lead to its own brand of spirituality with an intense set of accompanying practices. But it is jealous of its secrets and committed to its ways. It doesn't tell you how to move from its tight intellectual and spiritual structure into the freedom of the formless unknown. This you must accomplish for yourself. There is a way, and it is contained in a technique.

At the root of your consciousness, beneath your realities, ideas, feelings and intentions, is a certainty that connects you to the mystery of your origins. This certainty has a voice, and if you're quiet enough you can hear it. You can learn to ask this certainty any question you have about your own nature, and its voice will answer you. If you can hear the answer, you can believe it. It won't fail you and it is never wrong.

The technique for reaching this certainty is called contemplation. You can learn it. If you do, it will set you free. You will then forever have your own guide to your own truth with which you can test and judge any teaching. Eventually, it can become a compass to guide you through the unknown, where there are neither teachers nor explanations.

Like the systems of esotericism, the technique of contemplation is usually attached to a spirituality with a strong gravitational attraction. That's where you normally go to learn it. But unlike esoteric knowledge, contemplation has a bias toward freedom. Learn it, make it your primary practice, dive into it deeply, and in time it will make you your own master.

Contemplation teaches you to turn your attention, and your questions, inward. Contemplation of tarot will teach you to become tarot. All that you learn from esoteric knowledge and practice will come alive in you as you.

To accomplish this is a great, rare and worthy thing. On this level, tarot is no longer a deck of cards. That's where tarot starts, but not where it either begins or ends. Beginning and end are not start and finish. Tarot, like everything else, begins and ends where limit has not yet been created. Tarot turned inward moves toward its own origins in the unknowable.

As it does so, its symbols—names, numbers, images, and archetypes—become a language that you speak, a matrix with which you reassemble the world that you experience. What you actually see and hear and feel will remain the same as always. What you make of it all will be quite, quite different. Without ever lifting your feet from the ground of reality, you may find other worlds rising around you. When this happens, the level of excitement, interest, power and freedom in your life rises exponentially.

All of this is gradual, but the change is noticeable over time. For us, it is an exciting process. For you, it might or might not be an enticing prospect. Everyone who discovers these possibilities reacts to them in his or her own way.

Turning tarot, and yourself, inward is something of an adventure, and something of a romance. For some, its lure is irresistible. Others can take it or leave it. If the prospect of such an adventure is attractive but makes you a bit nervous, not to worry. For a very long time it tends to be a path filled with pleasure and with nothing to fear. There's a lot to learn and a lot to do that would make you continuously better and stronger. Your tarot would improve dramatically along the way and everyone, including yourself, would benefit from it. Your whole life would change for the better.

There's another comforting thing to consider. Each person turns tarot inward in his or her own way. We do it from an armchair and a computer. Others travel. Some find hidden and amazing teachers. There really are great traditions of secret knowledge possessed by communities tucked away in odd corners, sometimes within walking distance, that you can find if that's your fancy.

The world you know is much stranger than you think. And there are more worlds than you can see, right in front of your eyes. Tarot turned inward can show you all of this, and take you to where it can be found.

At the very beginning of this article, we spoke of saving tarot from its previous incarnations while leaving all of them in place. Such "salvations" are usually accomplished by intriguing the tarot public with something new and compelling, something made of a combination of history, current experience, and imagination.

Tarot turned inward is like that. It uses centuries-old knowledge and techniques that are easy to find when you are ready to look. It is compatible with the most informed kind of contemporary experience. And it imagines a path of great possibility, arising from what we know and leading into a fertile future.

Whether it is a possibility that will seize your imagination remains to be seen. But we offer it with faith and knowledge, love and respect, and with all our hearts.

Past-Life Tarot

by Mark McElroy

Do you believe you've lived before?

At a party I attended in 2006, I met a middle-aged man who claimed to have recovered memories of a past life. After dinner, he pushed back his plate of bread pudding and announced, "In a former life, I was a black woman. I clearly recall giving birth to a baby in the middle of a cotton field behind the railroad tracks."

Earlier the same year, I met a woman known for her ability to help others glimpse their past lives. She darted around the room, peering into people's eyes and announcing what she saw: "You were a fish. Yes, definitely a fish. And you—you were a horse. And you? You were a dancer in Russia, but you starved to death before you could make your first performance."

I've also met a young man who very quietly recounts his own past-life story: "I dream about this place constantly," he says. "I lived in a muddy, rutted village. We were always cold and usually hungry. There was something wrong with my teeth; I was always in pain. There's another man there—overweight and dirty and ragged. We work together, but, at some point, he kills me in an argument over food."

In 2005, ABC News covered the dramatic tale of James Leininger, a six-year-old boy believed by his family to be the reincarnation

✦
✳ of James M. Huston, Jr., a World War II fighter pilot. A number of
✦ people, including Huston's own sister, have been convinced by the
vivid details Leininger seems to recall of his life and death.

Some people believe stories like these are proof of the reality of reincarnation. Others insist that "reclaimed memories" are nothing more than half-remembered dreams or vivid fantasies. While I don't claim to have all the answers, I do know this: if you're interested in exploring the idea of past lives, your tarot deck is a powerful tool for doing so.

Reincarnation: A Secret Teaching of the Tarot?

Reincarnation has long been one of the esoteric tarot's "hidden teachings." Over the years, many writers have equated the Fool with themes of life, death, and rebirth. Kabbalistic systems often equate the Fool with Kether, the crown and "The Source of Life"—an assignment that suggests the Fool's descent from the world of potential into the world of distilled physical forms.

Many readers equate the pack over the shoulder of the *Rider-Waite-Smith* (RWS) Fool as the repository of memories and wisdom collected during previous lives. The Fool's number—when he's given a number at all—is usually zero, a number whose shape suggests the idea of endless cycles. And, of course, there is the Major Arcana itself, which can be seen as a circular expression of Joseph Campbell's "hero's journey": the Fool begins as a callow youth, survives the twenty-one tests represented by the other Majors, achieves the integration and enlightenment suggested by the World, and then begins the journey anew.

Reincarnation, then, would appear to be woven into the fabric of the modern esoteric tarot. That fact, combined with tarot's unique ability to tap thoughts, memories, and stories long submerged in the subconscious, makes the deck a powerful tool for exploring past lives.

Gentle Words of Caution

If you plan to work with tarot as part of an effort to illuminate past lives, please keep the following cautions in mind:

- Past-life exploration is a serious venture. Attempts to peer into previous lives should not be taken lightly. Proceed with this exercise only if you feel a compelling need to make a connection with a prior self.

- Not all past lives are pleasant ones. Repressed memories (whether forged in your current or your previous lives) have often been buried for a reason.

- Past lives often don't "perform on demand." As a result of dreamwork or meditative regression, you may wish to explore a specific incarnation. The details uncovered by this exercise may relate to that existence . . . or come from another. Be open to whatever insights occur.

- Not everyone can be Helen of Troy. While you may fancy having been the "face that launched a thousand ships," you may connect with a fairly mundane prior existence. Fame is not necessarily an indicator of a successful incarnation. The insights you achieved as a lowly shopkeeper may be more important than those achieved in a more high-profile previous life.

Stepping Back

This process for reviewing a prior existence is simple but powerful. I recommend you perform this experiment only when you have a minimum of one hour to pursue it; otherwise, you may rush through the steps and neglect important insights.

Step One: Preparation

Prepare for this reading by grounding and centering yourself using whatever tradition you honor. Turn off cell phones, telephones, televisions, and other distractions. Do whatever must be done to avoid interruptions during this work. The experiment may be undertaken in any setting; however, you may find it useful to dim the lights, light candles, play meditative music, or burn incense. You should feel protected, empowered, and safe.

Step Two: Meditation on the Fool

From whatever deck you prefer, remove the Fool (or its equivalent). Once you are seated comfortably on the floor, take the card in both hands and focus on the illustration. Clear your mind. When distracting thoughts occur, acknowledge them, tell them, "I'll deal with you later," and return your attention to the card.

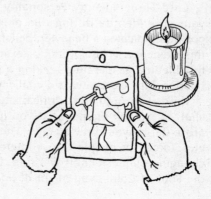

✦ With time, your focus will soften or your eyes will grow heavy.
✳ When this occurs, allow your eyes to close—but maintain the image
✦ of the Fool card in your mind. Think of this image as a frame of film.
When you feel ready, prompt your "inner projectionist" to play the
card's "movie" in reverse.

If you are working with the RWS Fool, the young man in the illustration will walk slowly backward. The clouds above him will retreat toward the distant horizon. The rose he carries will revert from blossom to bud. The white dog at his feet will cavort in reverse.

Keep your inner eye on the Fool as he shrinks from your field of view. When you can no longer see him, allow the image of the card to slowly fade to black.

Step Three: The Reading
Gently open your eyes. Replace the Fool in the deck and shuffle it. Beginning at the top, deal eight cards into an upright column: three cards above, two crossed cards in the center, and three cards below.

Card One: Your Gender. This card holds clues to your gender during a past life. Don't obsess on the apparent gender of the character in the illustration. While this may be an indicator of your previous gender, the really important question to ask is this: what gender do you *feel* the card symbolically suggests?

Card Two: Your Family. This card indicates something of importance about the family into which you were born. The Ten of Cups may suggest a large, happy, loving environment. The Justice card may point to a strict, sterile household where rules were more important than freedom. The Eight of Cups may suggest that something was missing from your home environment, and could be read as anything from "an absent parent" to "life as an only child."

Card Three: Identity/Personality. This card provides insight into your core identity during this previous lifetime. A Major in this position indicates a behavior, belief, or world view that dominated this existence. (The Lovers, for example, might indicate you spent this lifetime desperately seeking a soulmate . . . or that romantic relationships were always a challenge for you.)

Cards Four and Five: Critical Situation. These cards are a snapshot—a "Kodak moment," if you like—of a critical situation that arose during your previous life. The two cards represent two energies, forces, or people whose interactions created a climax of life-changing dimensions. If you find the Eight of Wands paired with the Four of Coins, you might decide your previous self received a sudden insight (Eight of Wands) that prompted him to save food and money (Four of Coins) in preparation for a coming disaster.

Card Six: Response. This card represents the all-important response you made to the crisis defined by cards Four and Five. The Devil in this position might indicate that the fellow from our previous example hoarded his provisions for himself; the Six of Coins, though, might suggest that he endeared himself to others by freely sharing his resources.

Card Seven: Life Lesson. This card symbolizes the life lesson you learned during this existence. Expect this card to refer, at least in part, to the crisis outlined in cards Four and Five and the response signified by card Six. The Tower in this position, for example, might indicate that, as a result of being led to help others, you learned to escape the prison of obsessive self-interest.

Card Eight: Influence on Your Present Life. This card will reveal how the existence depicted in this spread colors your thoughts, feelings, emotions, and choices today. The King of Swords in this position could suggest that your cool handling of a past-life crisis prepared you to be a present-day leader. On the other hand, the Two of Wands might suggest today's inability to stick with a course of action is rooted in self-doubt left over from a previous incarnation's self-doubt.

Step Four: Follow-Up

Knowing about a past life is one thing; knowing how to use this information to foster positive change and growth is another.

Once you have genuinely opened yourself to the revelations of this reading, collect all the cards, shuffle them, and draw three new cards, placing them in a simple horizontal line.

Card One: Honoring the Past. This card suggests something you can do today as a means of acknowledging the work you performed in the past. The Four of Swords might prompt you to offer a short prayer for the person you were, or the Star card might lead you to make a libation—a small offering of wine or water, poured out over an altar of small stones—in recognition of a former self.

Card Two: Putting Wisdom to Work. This card suggests a way you can put your past life experience to work today. If you discover, for example, that you worked as a successful craftsman in the past, drawing the Eight of Coins might encourage you to take up a handicraft you could use to enhance present-day income.

Card Three: Looking Forward. Reconnecting with past lives can be exciting, but your present life has lessons of its own to teach!

✦ This card, which hints at your current life's agenda, will suggest
✳ a matter in the present that requires your attention. (Drawing the
✦ Hierophant, for example, might motivate you to schedule more time
for deliberate spiritual practice.) Pondering how this card extends
or builds upon your past life experience will be both satisfying and
enlightening.

Additional Tips for Past-Life Explorers

- Take some time to explore the insights suggested by this
  reading. Expect connections among cards to reveal themselves in subtle ways. One good way to expand and
  preserve the information you gather during this exercise is
  to translate it into a journal entry by writing a paragraph or
  two about each card.

- Want to explore a specific past life you've glimpsed before?
  Choose cards deliberately to represent what you *do* know;
  draw random cards to "fill in the blanks" and complete the
  picture.

- If some cards remain inscrutable, or if you feel uncertain
  about the information you receive, you can always
  supplement your insights with commentary cards:
  additional cards drawn to amplify or enhance the meaning
  of the original card. Place commentary cards to the right
  of the cards they modify; they will "extend" the story and
  allow you to glimpse additional details.

- Even if your current beliefs do not embrace reincarnation,
  this spread can still provide you with a great deal of insight.
  After "generating" a past life with the cards, try interpreting
  the story you've created as though it were a symbolic
  dream. What truths about your present life might this "past-
  life experience" reveal?

Plant Symbolism

by Mary K. Greer

Many symbols on the tarot cards are of plants: flowers, shrubs, trees, fruits, leaves, seeds, and grains. Plants are our relations, and vital to our existence and well-being. They soak up solar energy fire and transform it through photosynthesis into several kinds of fuel. They turn inorganic compounds into organic ones, and create oxygen, which all animals must breathe to live. In Greek, Vedic, Indonesian, and some American Indian lore, plants manifest as gods, expressing purposes and qualities related to the plant characteristics. Interaction with plants can make us feel closer to heaven. Cultivated plants grow in gardens, resulting in public and personal enjoyment and signifying the establishment of the heavenly garden on Earth. They represent the growth of knowledge and ability. As scents, plants stimulate emotions, as medicines they heal the body and mind, as foods they nurture us, and their products protect and sustain us. They can also poison and kill. Recognize the message in plants and you will understand what is feeding you, sheltering you, and mirroring your emotions and spirit.

Early tarot decks used few plants on the Major Arcana. In 1781 Antoine Court de Gébelin announced in the third volume of *Le Monde Primitif* (his encyclopedia on the remains of an earlier "golden age" society) that esoteric meanings were found in the cards. Plants were deliberately added to the cards to make certain allusions more obvious. The *Rider-Waite-Smith* tarot (1909), in its oft-imitated illustrations of the Minor Arcana, especially focused on plants as symbols. In the following discussion the author will therefore be referring to this deck unless otherwise stated.

We will begin with the Fool. Ivy appears on his robe, representing the vital life and immortality of the evergreen. It may point to the Fool's relationship to Bacchus or Dionysius, since ivy's cooling qualities were thought to cure the drunkenness for which these gods were famous. But more likely it represents their use of ivy to tenaciously draw worshipers into the divine frenzy of their mad dance. Ivy also presages death, since it is poisonous and draws vital moisture from trees. Remaining green long after the tree is dead, it represents life-out-of-death. Thus the Fool, with hints of divine madness, represents the soul that continues after the death of the body.

The white rose, representing purity and innocence, appears many times in the tarot: first, in the hand of the Fool, where its fragrance is his guide. Later in the deck comes Death, carrying a banner emblazoned with a white rose. In both cards, the rose represents desire and passion, as do all roses, but being white it is pure and innocent—the desire of the soul for perfection, passionately yearning for union with the divine. Its singularity emphasizes the single focus of desire in both cards. In the Death card, with its perfect mandala shape, the rose also represents completion. Roses in general are a Hermetic sign of secrecy and silence. Supposedly the Great Goddess gave a rose to Harpocrates, the Egyptian god of silence, to keep him from revealing the secret of eternal life. It represents her gift of sexuality as the source of all creation.

Red roses speak of instinct, passion, and the fiery spirit, while white lilies stand for intellect, purity, and the peaceful soul. In the legends of the Virgin Mary's immaculate conception by her mother Anne, and again in her own virgin conception of

IL MATTO / LE FOU 0 THE FOOL / EL LOCO

DER NARR DE DWAAS

The Fool from *The Universal Tarot*

the Christ-child, it was the smelling of a rose and a lily, respectively, that achieved the miracles. The flowers usually appear together to balance the dual energies characterized as whore and maiden, sexuality and innocence, desire and intellect, will and imagination, blood and milk, Sun and Moon.

Roses and lilies are the most prevalent plants in the tarot, adapted by magicians to represent the requirements of magic. The Magician must cultivate the five roses before him—representing the five senses (source of all desires)—as well as the four lilies representing the four elements (or worlds of abstract thought). The Hierophant recognizes these drives in his two acolytes, for the robe of one is covered in roses and the other in lilies, and as teacher the Hierophant must speak to the needs of each.

Florence Farr, a chief in the Hermetic Order of the Golden Dawn from which both the *Rider-Waite-Smith* and the *Thoth* decks evolved, explained in *Euphrates or the Waters of the East* the magical views represented by the rose and lily: "The sun and moon are the celestial luminaries, but the central ones are a fire hidden in the earth or *nitre*, and an airy lunar nature in the water. These two mixed natures are known to us as the desires of the flesh [rose] and the phantasies of the imagination [lily]: in their transmutation by consecration of the desires [rose] and purification of the thoughts [lily], lies the pathway to wisdom. The will [rose] and the imagination [lily] of an adept are symbolized by the Urim and Thummin of the High Priest."

These same two flowers also appear on several Minor Arcana cards: in the Two of Wands, the rose and lily are crossed, representing the choice facing the initiate. We return to the roses and lilies found in the garden of the Magician in the Ace of Pentacles, where, with the knowledge gained on our journey through the tarot, we may choose to remain in the garden of earthly experience or leave through the gate into the unknown. Lilies supposedly sprang from the tears of Eve when she was expelled from the Garden of Eden, as memories of her lost innocence.

Additionally, red roses appear in Strength as a garland linking the maiden with the lion (her desire-nature); in a sense the maiden is the lily and the lion is the rose. Red roses in the shape of a Venus symbol (representing love) appear on the gown of the Empress, while red roses on the quilt of the Nine of Swords promise that in time (the checkerboard signs of the zodiac) the nightmare of depression will transform back into a desire for life.

A full-blown white lily to the Empress's left in Oswald Wirth's tarot deck, created in the 1880s, shows how enthralling in its purity is her charm, gentleness, and beauty. In the Emperor the lily has become the stylized fleur-de-lys used by royalty to express the force of idealism, nobility of soul, and true generosity that rises and spreads like the Sun.

Wirth used the red tulip flower as an evolving symbol of spiritual hope and development in his deck. In the Magician it appears as a bud showing an early stage of initiation. The red tulip fully opens in response to the vital energy of the Emperor. By Temperance the flower has begun to droop, but the angelic cup-bearer revives it with fertilizing rains or morning dew. Wirth further explains that the refreshing intervention of Temperance "restores new sap to the vegetable overpowered by the ripening heat of Leo." The tulip still blooms as the Fool steps blindly over it in the next-to-last card of Wirth's deck, indicating that active spirituality will never abandon the innocent, no matter how irresponsible and unseeing they are. Tarot clients sometimes identify their soul-self with this simple and humble flower, unobtrusively awaiting our notice.

Embroidered on the veil behind the High Priestess are palm trees and pomegranates. Palms are phallic symbols indicating archetypal masculine virility. They also represent the spine. Pomegranates symbolize female fertility for their many seeds, as well as the red womb and the heart. The Hebrew name for pomegranate, *rimmon*, means "to bear a child." At least one tradition names pomegranates as the forbidden fruit in the Garden of Eden.

Cypresses are symbolic of both death and rebirth. In the Empress card they represent solace and comfort offered by a woman of maturity, and remind us how close birth is to death—that the new life the pregnant Empress carries is born to die.

The apple tree behind the woman on the Lovers card represents earthly desires and fecundity. It is the Tree of Knowledge of Good and Evil. Although the Bible does not mention apples, they probably became known as the fruit of temptation because the pentagram pattern created by the pips (representing spiritual humanity) was encased in the flesh of earth-bound passions and pleasures. Apples appear in many myths as a reward given to the woman of greatest allure and beauty, but it is always a choice that comes with a price. For instance, just as Eve's choice resulted in the fall from the Garden, so Troy fell as a result of Paris awarding the apple to Aphrodite. Five apples on the tree signify the five physical senses that became, after the fall, our mode of perception, our primary way of gaining knowledge.

The flame-tree behind the man in the Lovers is the Tree of Life, pictured as a resinous tree like the sacred frankincense or myrrh, burning its fragrant incense in sacrifice to the gods.

An ash tree, reminiscent of the World Tree, Yggdrasil, on which Odin hung himself, is featured on the Hanged Man card, where it represents magical sacrifice.

The iris flower on the Temperance card represents Iris, the cup-bearer of the gods and handmaiden of Hera, who, as the rainbow, was guide for the souls of women.

Traditionally the bush in the background of the Star card is an acacia, which has a long magical tradition. Sacred to the Egyptians, since it remains green even in the desert, it affirms our hope in reincarnation, the soul, and immortality. Blossoming simultaneously both white and red, it combines the symbolism of the red and white roses, and the red rose and white lily. According to Paul Foster Case, the bush represents the human brain and nervous system, and on it perches the ibis—the symbol of Thoth, the Egyptian god of learning and magic.

In Freemasonry, the evergreen acacia reveals the location of the tomb of the Master of Wisdom; thus the discerning seeker can uncover buried truths. Surrounding the pond are ten tiny flowers that could be violets, since they represent the transitory qualities of life made apparent to us during mystical meditation; they also induce sleep. They may also represent the maidens transformed into flowers by Cupid to hide them from Aphrodite's jealousy of their beauty.

Sunflowers appear on the Sun card. They are abundant with seeds and thus the potential for rebirth, and represent the radiant life energy that heliotropically turns toward the One. Sunflowers also appear on the Queen of Wands, where the gold flower represents haughtiness and pride, together with reasoned perception—the ability of this Queen to shed light on all issues.

Evergreen wreaths appear frequently in the deck, and may be of myrtle or bay laurel. The Empress, Fool, and woman in the Two of Cups are probably crowned with myrtle wreaths, while the Charioteer and the champion in the Six of Wands are, more likely, wearing laurel wreaths. Additional wreaths depend from the wand of the victor in the Six of Wands, and arise from a cup in the Seven of Cups. Myrtle was sacred to Aphrodite and Astarte as a sign of immortality and promise of resurrection. The Greeks used it to crown bloodless victors and designate authority. Awarded to poets, it signified that their fame would remain ever green. The laurel, on the other hand, was sacred to Apollo, but similarly denoted victory, success, and fame everlasting. Additionally, it was associated with prophecy.

The wreath surrounding the dancer in the World card is, I believe, of myrtle. In nineteenth-century Italian decks there is a wreath of flowers, representing the fragrant aura, the "odor of sanctity" mentioned in the Bible, which charms and exalts the soul. Myrtle, sacred to the Goddess, was the chief scented tree in the Garden of Eden. According to an Arabic myth, God allowed Adam and Eve to take it with them so that its fragrance would remind them of resurrection, love, and immortality.

The garland of fruit and flowers in the Four of Wands, and the profusion of grapes, pumpkins, oranges, and apples in the Three of Cups, represent harvest, bounty, nurturing, sharing, and fertility—as do the pears and apples in the Queen of Pentacles.

A palm frond and a sprig of myrtle (complete with berries) drape from the pierced crown of the Ace of Swords. The image here is of the Kabbalistic Tree of Life—comprising ten sephiroth (or "sapphires" of light)—of which the three highest are pictorially represented: *Kether* (Crown—indicated literally by a crown), *Chokmah* (Wisdom, and the Pillar of Mercy—indicated by the palm frond), and *Binah* (Understanding, and the Pillar of Severity—indicated by the myrtle sprig). The sword itself signifies the Middle Pillar of the Tree. Historically, the palm was awarded to victorious gladiators in Rome, and the myrtle to successful generals.

Water lilies appear in the Ace of Cups and on the robe of the Page of Cups, and the *Thoth* deck features the water lily or lotus on the Cups cards and several others. The water lily traditionally blends solar and lunar consciousness—the center is the Sun (or son) surrounded by the feminine petals. Rooted in mud, it rises through the life-waters of the unconscious and opens in the air to receive the life of the Sun, which releases the flower's heavenly aroma. As the favorite scent of the Egyptians, the lotus represents the quintessence. Signifying creativity and spiritual evolution, in the Thoth deck especially, the condition and color of the lotuses indicate the creative, vital, and spiritual state described by the particular card.

The mythical pentacle or "money bush" appears in the Seven of Pentacles, looking nothing like the official money plant (lunaria). In the *Motherpeace Tarot*, we find a pumpkin vine substituted, echoing the roundness of the very pregnant woman also depicted. The reference in both is to the patience and trust needed for overcoming the fears and anxieties that come while waiting for the fruits of one's labors to ripen.

The Six of Cups features a white star-flower in each cup (a giant star jasmine, a wild white rose, a white periwinkle?). But the images also represent the enclosed garden—as in the Song of Solomon where: "A garden enclosed is my sister, my spouse, a spring shut up, a fountain sealed." The children are, at least metaphorically, brother and sister, and still innocent as the white flower implies. Interestingly, the enclosed garden of the Nine of Pentacles represents, with its hanging grapes, the mature, voluptuous, and fertile female, while that of the Ace of Pentacles offers an open gateway to new experience.

Oak leaves, sacred to thunder-and-lightning gods like Zeus and Thor, top the helmet of the Knight of Pentacles (and his horse), indicating that he is the Oak King or Green Man. In Rome, oak leaves were a sign of service to the state, or awarded for saving the life of a citizen, representing endurance and strength.

Bunches of grapes and vines of grape leaves are found on the robes of the King of Pentacles and the old man in the Ten of Pentacles. The wall of the Nine of Pentacles is also covered in grapes. Grapes are ambivalent. They represent both fertility/new life and blood/sacrifice. In these three cards, they depict wealth and a rich, full life—but with a hint of recognition that this is merely a fleeting experience in the face of deeper truths. The additional meaning of intoxication implies an intoxication with life.

Finally, two small red flowers blossom on the tree of life in the stained glass window in the Five of Pentacles, promising that spring will follow the cold of winter.

At their most general, flowers represent our emotions and spirituality; trees act as a spine, axis, or ladder connecting the underworld to Earth to heaven; evergreens denote immortality; leaves express

◆ new life, vitality and growth; fruits indicate abundance and wealth;
✳ seeds signify fertility and potential; grains suggest a neverending
◆ cycle of death and resurrection; roots give us a secure contact with
Earth and suggest nurturance; while branches reach into the sky in
an attitude of aspiration and inspiration.

Tarot and Death

Part Two

by Nina Lee Braden

Since I discovered tarot in 1990, it has become woven into the very fabric of my life, so when my father died in March of 2005, I began a study of death by using the tarot. In other words, I used the tarot to help me with my grieving process. It was most timely that I did so, for in the months to follow, death seemed my constant companion. My uncle, two aunts, a cousin, and friends died. Most significantly, my only sibling, my younger brother, tragically died from injuries sustained in a motorcycle accident. As a result of all of this loss, my mother became increasingly frail, and I had to take responsibility for her care. Without the aid of the tarot, I don't know how I would have survived the season of death. Even with the tarot, the season of death has been the most difficult time of my life.

When I began my study of tarot and death, I did not study alone. As I so frequently do, I took along my friends and students. I taught a series of three two-hour classes on tarot and death. We explored the concept of death in a variety of ways, and in each way, we also included the tarot.

Death Avoidance?

In our modern society, many of us are uncomfortable even saying the word "death." In our current society, most of us are not very

exposed to death. This was true for me until the last several years. During my season of death, when I had so many friends and family members die, I was geographically far away from most of them and only found out afterward about their deaths. Until 1998, I had never been with a person as he or she died, and in our society, this is not unusual. However, I was at my brother's side through-out a sixteen-day hospital stay, and I sang to him and kissed him as he died. I was with my great-aunt each day for several days as she slowly died at age ninety-two.

Since death is so uncomfortable for many of us, we have developed euphemisms. We don't say, "He died." Instead, we say, "He's gone to heaven," or "she passed over." I used this habit of euphemizing death for another interactive activity with my students. We brainstormed as many euphemisms for death and dying as we could think of. Some of them included: the man's been here, deceased, terminated, went to a better place, passed on, shuffled off, gone to the great blue yonder, passed away, gone to the undiscovered country, gone to his reward, gone to heaven, bought the farm, transitioned, expired, harvested, gone to the eternal care unit, croaked, crossed over, kicked the bucket, gave up the ghost, gone to meet the maker, gone to the great hereafter, called home, and gone to the pearly gates.

Each of these presents a slightly different view of death and the afterlife. We then choose tarot cards to represent various choices. Would you use the same tarot card to represent "the man's been here" and "shuffled off"? Would you use the same card for "croaked" and "called home"? To me, "gone to the undiscovered country" would be the Fool. "Gone to heaven" would be Judgement. "Harvested" and "bought the farm" would be the Empress. "Gone to a better place" would be the Star. Which cards would you use? Why? Does assigning tarot cards for the euphemisms reinforce the denial or strip it away?

Fifty Ways to Die

Paul Simon sings that there are fifty ways to leave your lover, but are there fifty ways to die? How many ways can you think of? Quick—before reading further, get a pen and paper and jot down as many ways to die as you can think of. How many did you get?

My students and I brainstormed on ways to die, and we filled a white board with all of these causes of death. It became obvious that there was a wide variety of ways to die. No one card, not even the Death card, could adequately depict all of these methods of dying. Might perhaps another card better depict a type of death? For example, drowning might better be depicted by either Judgement or the Hanged Man. Electrocution might better be depicted by the Magician and so on. We started matching different tarot cards to the different causes of death. Would you choose a different card for sudden infant death syndrome and falling from airplane without a parachute? Would you choose a different card for gunshot and drowning? Which cards would you choose? Why?

When we finished with this exercise, we were surprised by the cards that did not come up. Obviously, the Ten of Swords was a great choice for death by stabbing. The Tower was the clear choice for death by falling from a great height. However, a number of cards did not come up at all for anyone.

Every card in the tarot deck can depict death under the right circumstances, so I decided to shuffle my deck and deal ten cards off the top. What kind of death could I see from the Six of Cups? Sudden infant death syndrome. What about the Sun, that happiest and most radiant of cards? Heat stroke. The Empress? Death in childbirth. What cards do you draw? What type of death can you assign to each one?

I took this exercise one step further. What message about death could each card bring me? The Death card is not the only card to teach of death. Each of the seventy-eight cards can reveal a message about death, dying, and grieving. Temperance tells me that death is a part of the cycle of life. The Nine of Pentacles tells me that each of us dies alone even if we are surrounded by others. The Four of Pentacles tells me that we can't take our material possessions with us when we die. The Ace of Cups tells me that there can be love and beauty in death. What message about death can you see in each card?

The Opposite of Death

One way to study something is to examine its opposite. I asked my class, "What is the opposite of death?" Often there is a transition period before death, a time when we are technically alive but our bodies and souls have definitely started on the journey to the undiscovered country. When we are on that road, death is not our opposite, so it is not always accurate to say that life is the opposite of death. My class had several good suggestions: radiance, dynamism, vigor, vibrancy, energy, and vitality. We then each chose a card to represent what was, to us, the opposite of death. I see the opposite of death as vitality, and so I chose the Sun as the opposite of death, but any number of other cards would work. There is no one right answer—there are many right answers. What do you see as the opposite of death? What card would you choose to represent it? What card would you use to represent life?

Occupations of Death

Drawing on astrology, my students and I tried another exercise about death. In astrology, the Eighth House is the house of death, but it also represents professions that deal with death. My class tried to come up with as many occupations/places of employment associated with death as possible, and then chose cards for these occupations. What card writes obituaries? What card is the medical examiner? What card is a grief counselor? Choices will vary from individual to individual, depending on how you see the jobs and how you see the cards themselves. I might choose the Page of Swords as the writer of obituaries, the King of Swords as the medical examiner, and the High Priestess as the grief counselor, but you could also choose, respectively, the Seven of Swords, the Three of Pentacles, and the Queen of Cups.

Not only does this exercise expand our thinking about occupations that deal with death, but it also expands our concepts of the cards. If you see the Knight of Pentacles as an exterminator, you may find yourself giggling over mental pictures of dead termites the next time you read a description of the Knight of Pentacles as stiff and wooden. If you see the High Priestess as a grief counselor, you may modify your concept of her as always being aloof and unflappable.

Stages of Grief Spread

Tarot can teach us not only about death but about grief. Many people say that there are five stages of grief: denial, anger, bargaining, depression, and acceptance. During my season of death, since I suffered so many losses at once, I would often find myself going through several different stages simultaneously, each about the loss of a different person. For example, when I heard that a longtime email friend and mentor had died unexpectedly, I was in the first stage of grief: denial. However, at the same time, I was in the final stage of acceptance over my father's death and in the anger stage over my brother's death.

If you are working through any type of grief (and we can grieve over failed relationships, the loss of a job, or many other things, not only a death), you might want to try this simple spread based on the five stages of grief. This spread presupposes that you may be simultaneously experiencing more than one stage at a time. I lay out the cards in a vertical column, with Card One at the bottom and Card Five at the top, indicating a climb up. At the top of the spread, I lay the final card horizontally, to show completion.

Card One: I am denying _____.

Card Two: I am angry about _____.

Card Three: I want to bargain to achieve _____.

Card Four: I am depressed because _____.

Card Five: I can accept my loss and begin to _____.

Card Six: I choose to live with _____.

Final Words

In a way, what I did with my classes on tarot and death was to see that any card can portray a truth about death. So, although death and Death are paired, what I tried to do was to *un*pair them and to show that almost any card can be associated with death.

I ended my final class on tarot and death by having everyone go through his or her deck, face-up, and choose the card that represented a personal concept of death. (Some chose two cards, one for death and one for the afterlife.) How do you see death? What card would you choose to represent it? Why?

My students and I went around the room and shared our cards. My personal choice was the Fool because I see death as one more great adventure (Hamlet's "undiscovered country"). Frankly, although suffering frightens me terribly, death itself holds no fear for me. Fear and death, although frequently confused, are not the same thing, and we certainly fear things other than death. What card do you most associate with fear? How does it depict your fear? My card choice for fear changes from time to time, but the Tower is one that I come back to frequently. I find that living with the fear of the Tower is an ongoing challenge.

◆   I have much living to do, much more to experience, but when
✳ my time comes, I hope that I will be as eager to explore the undis-
◆ covered country of death as I have been eager to explore the new
154 adventures of life. Let me be the Fool in life and the Fool in death,
     stepping boldly off the edge of the cliff into the great unknown.

An Evening with the High Priestess

by James Ricklef

There is a popular impression that the tarot is only a tool for divination, but it has other valuable uses as well. A very effective one is the use of a tarot card to facilitate a guided visualization, which is a process that opens our consciousness to messages from our intuition, and this is what we will explore here.

A guided visualization is like a waking dream that is directed with specific intent, usually by way of a script (which makes it somewhat like an imaginary movie). It also can be thought of as a bridge that spans the gulf between the conscious, rational mind and the subconscious, intuitive mind. Thus, it allows us to explore new ideas and feelings, and it does so in a symbolic way, which helps us feel more comfortable as we examine points of view that we might find threatening or frightening if presented more directly. Also, as we shall see in this article, the tarot is a wonderful catalyst for this process since our subconscious mind communicates through the use of signs, symbols, and metaphorical images—much like the tarot does.

Preparations

Before beginning a guided visualization, you should decide what you want to accomplish with it. Is there a problem or issue in your life you need help with? Do you need healing for yourself or maybe

for a relationship? Or are you seeking a general exploration of what
is going on in your life right now?

You also should determine what you want to do in the course of
the visualization. For example, do you want to ask the person in the
card a specific question or request advice from him or her? Maybe
you would like the person in the card to guide you on an imaginary
journey that can serve as a metaphorical exploration of your life. In
any case, it is essential to put together a clear plan, which takes the
form of a script for your visualization.

You must realize, however, that sometimes a guided visualization
will veer off onto an unexpected tangent as if directed by an unseen
hand. If so, allow the process free rein and see where it takes you,
for your subconscious mind usually has a better idea of what you
need right now than your rational mind. As an analogy, consider
that although it is a good idea to prepare a map and itinerary prior
to going on a trip, some of the most interesting experiences are to be
had on accidental side trips.

Finally, since your eyes will be closed during this meditative process, it is impossible to read your visualization script while following this procedure. You can memorize the basic steps beforehand as
best you can, and then stay true to the script's general intent, if not
to every precise detail. This option requires passable memorization
skills, but you do not need to learn the script verbatim. Or if you
have a friend who can help you, she or he can read the script to
you while you do the meditation. However, this friend should have
a good grasp of the purpose of the script and of how to pace the
reading of it. Or, you can record the script on tape or CD and let the
recording direct you through the process.

Beginning

In preparation for a guided visualization, you must first enter a
peaceful state of mind, and the following relaxation technique will
help you do so. (Of course, if there is another process that you
prefer, feel free to use that instead.) The purpose of this step is to
silence the droning chatter of your conscious mind in order to allow
the quiet, subtle voice of your intuition to come through.

First, get comfortable. Pick a time when you are unlikely to be
disturbed and when you can eliminate any source of distraction.
(For example, be sure to turn off your cell phone.) Some people prefer to do meditative work in total silence, but others like to have
soothing music playing softly in the background. Find what works
for you. Also, dim the lights and find a comfy chair to sit in.

Once you are comfortable, begin to breathe slowly and deeply, and continue to do so until your breath is deep, rhythmic, and natural. Then as you feel increasingly calm and serene, imagine a beam of white light shining down on you from above. See yourself enveloped in a warm, soothing cocoon of light and know that you are safe within it.

After a moment, look at the card you have chosen to use. Describe out loud its physical details: the people in it, the setting, the background, etc. Take note of what the people in the card are wearing and doing. What objects or symbols command your attention? Also, what mood or feeling does this card evoke in you?

Once you have done this, close your eyes and resume your deep, rhythmic breathing as you settle into a relaxed state. Then visualize the card in as much detail as possible, seeing it in your mind's eye as vividly as you can. Allow the image to become vibrant, and see the card grow until it becomes life-sized. See the borders around the card become a doorway leading into its scenery, and then imagine yourself stepping through that doorway and into the card itself.

You are now ready to proceed with your guided visualization script.

The High Priestess

To demonstrate this process, we will take a look at a sample visualization script that you can use with the High Priestess card. First, however, let's consider some general themes about this card as they apply to a guided visualization.

The High Priestess represents the mysteries of the subconscious as well as the unfathomable forces in our lives. Consequently, a guided visualization using this card may be particularly useful when there seems to be something mysterious going on in your life, or when you want to explore hidden motivations. It also can help you find the meaning of a perplexing dream that you recently had or that has been recurrent.

Many versions of the High Priestess card depict a woman holding a scroll as she sits in front of a veil stretched between two pillars, and these are potent symbols that can be incorporated into a

The High Priestess from *The Gilded Tarot*

THE HIGH PRIESTESS

visualization script. For example, you might begin by explaining to this priestess the problem, issue, or situation that brought you to her, and then listen to her read a relevant passage from her sacred book or scroll. You may clearly understand the significance of what she reads to you, or it might be enigmatic, its import not immediately obvious. In that case, you can discuss with her what she has read to you, and that discussion may shed some light on the subject.

Something else you can do is have the High Priestess invite you to walk with her behind the veil that hangs between the two pillars. When you go behind that veil, carefully observe what you find there. Is it a room, a landscape, a vast hall, the interior of a temple, or something else? You might want to let the priestess give you a tour, relying on her to show you the points of interest and to explain them to you. Alternatively, you may wander around alone, exploring whatever catches your attention, and then return to the High Priestess to discuss anything you did not understand.

What follows now is a script for a guided visualization with the High Priestess card, but keep in mind that it is merely a suggestion. You may want to modify it in order to create one that better suits your specific needs. Also, note that the characters "# # #" indicate a place where there should be a pause in the execution of the script.

A Guided Visualization

The first thing you notice as you enter this card is a serene woman seated before you. Her countenance is ageless, her expression inscrutable. You can see an ancient, almost eternal, wisdom in her eyes, but there is a strength and vitality in her form and demeanor that denies extreme age. Her pale blue robe flows about her and onto the floor like water, and when you look down, you notice that the marble tiles are wet and glistening. In fact, if you look closely, you may be able to see your face reflected in them.

The High Priestess asks you why you have come to her. As you answer her, she listens attentively and her gaze never wavers from your face.

# # #

When you have finished explaining your situation, she smiles knowingly and tells you that there is a passage in her book of ancient wisdom that will give you guidance. Reverently, she opens her book and reads to you in a melodious voice that captivates your attention.

# # #

When she has finished reading, she looks at you expectantly, patiently awaiting your response. Feel free to discuss with her what she has just read to you, asking for clarification or explanation of whatever you did not understand, and sharing your interpretations of the rest.

# # #

When you have finished this discussion, the High Priestess stands and gently sets down her book. She offers you her right hand as she draws back the veil behind her with her left hand, and she invites you into the temple beyond. You follow her into a large, beautiful room lit by hanging chandeliers, a thousand white candles blazing in each, and the two of you proceed toward the front of the temple where an ornate altar stands.

As you walk with the priestess, notice all that is around you: the intricate tile work beneath your feet, the beautiful paintings and decorations on the walls, and the ceiling's elaborately carved wood. Also, notice the scents and sounds in this vast hall. Can you smell a sweet aroma of incense? Can you hear the soothing murmur of chanting from somewhere in the distance? Drink in all that you observe without question or judgment, and when you approach the altar at the front of the temple, take note of each object on it so that you will be able to remember what it looks like later.

# # #

The High Priestess now motions you to sit as she moves behind the altar and turns to face you. She raises both of her hands, palms up, and as she does so a sparkling light shines down upon her, bathing her in a radiant glow. In a loud, clear voice, she proclaims that the ritual she is about to perform is one of illumination and discovery, and that it will draw forth from your soul the solution to your problem.

As you watch the High Priestess perform this ritual, it becomes indelibly etched upon your memory.

# # #

When the High Priestess has completed her ritual, she slowly walks toward you and beckons you to follow. You exit the temple with her, and she returns to her bench, her gaze once again impassive and enigmatic. Thank her for all that she has revealed to you, and then turn back toward the borders of the card and step out of it, leaving its imaginary landscape behind. Finally, watch the card shrink back to its normal size. It is again just a tarot card.

# # #

Take three deep breaths, and on the exhalation of each whisper your own name. When you are ready, open your eyes. Your guided visualization with the High Priestess card is now finished.

◆ **A Final Note**
✳
◆ Upon the completion of a guided visualization, it is important that
you immediately write down as much about it as you can, including your thoughts about what each of its elements meant to you.
This is because a guided visualization is like a dream in that if you
do not record it quickly, it will soon evaporate from your conscious
mind and be lost to you forever.

Bricks
of the Tower

by Elizabeth Hazel

Choosing to write about the Tower card was a bit risky. I started snooping into its mysteries and found myself tumbling off the parapets into the forbidden secrets of the ancients. Synapses fired and brain cells exploded. It was a Tower experience—albeit in the most positive sense. My views of the galaxy and ancient mythology were overthrown. The Tower revealed the roots of Time Zero, and nothing will ever be the same.

The intrinsic divinatory meaning of the Tower is chaos, destruction, and cataclysmic upheaval. Even when it is a spiritual awakening, the mind must still cope with being catapulted into an alien environment. An unquestioned prototype for the Tower's image is the Tower of Babel. The fate of this famous tower is a coded description of the ending of a World Age, and there are many of these. New gods do battle and overthrow the old gods; thus an old age is superseded by a new one. But who came up with the idea that the gods do battle at the turn of the ages? And when did it start?

Archeological evidence suggests that the awareness of shifting Aeons stretches back to unimaginable depths of prehistory, into the Paleolithic and Neolithic periods (30,000 to 3,000 BC). The ancient oral traditions from the Ages of Leo, Cancer, and Gemini were encapsulated in written records or in the relics of art and architecture during the Bronze Age (the Age of Taurus, around 4,000 to 3,000 BC). Each of the many diverse legends embodies the personality of a cultural period's fashion and tradition. We are heirs to a rich body of ancient literature that contains the World Age motif from Sumer, Greece, Persia, India, Finland, Iceland, China, and the early Americas.

World Age stories are amazingly Tower-like in both symbolism and content. The beauty of the code of the ancients is that the most profound magical lore is "history resistant." Its poetic incantations disguise knowledge in the cleverest ways, masking the principle galactic players in tales of conquest and adventure that seem little more than heroic feats of derring-do. The greatest themes are global and ubiquitous. Ancient astronomer-poets were anything but stupid, and did a clever job of hiding critical galactic information in appealing stories.

Stories about the Aeons lead into rivers of time and space. Gods making fire or cranking a churn make the old constellations fall "into the waters," and bring about the rising of the new. Tales about these critical moments in time represent a galactic transition called the precession of the equinoxes. These 2,400-year stellar shifts were known to the ancients, who carefully watched and recorded the movements of night skies. Through myth, they described the evidence of a dynamic connection between the shifting of stars and the shifting of civilizations. In their language, the ending of a World Age is the essence of primordial chaos, portrayed by gods in the heavens, and reflected by the upheaval of civilizations on Earth.

XVI The Tower

The Tower from *The Witches Tarot*

Existence revolves through repetitive patterns that are distinguished and embedded in the tarot. The Tower represents dynamic chaos—a worldview or structure wrenched apart by forces that strip away the stability of the existing structure. "Revolution" is a word of multivalent meaning. The planets make revolutions around the sun, and the solar system makes revolutions around the galaxy. This systemic revolution of galactic crossroads is at the heart of precession. Revolution is also a word that describes personal or cultural upheaval, a reaction to an obsolete government, system, or way of doing things that needs to be replaced with something new.

Revolutions, however cyclic and regular in astronomical, societal, or personal terms, bring changes that can't be undone. Some elements of the past, bricks from the Tower of the old cycle, can be salvaged, recycled, or reused. The mythic motifs and symbols that have survived through the ages are bricks that have had a makeover. Conquerors are good examples of the recycled material that survives Aeon shifts. They apply martial force to mold the world in their own image. They cause the Tower's downfall instead being victims of its forces. Legends of conquest also embody the applied brute energies of Mars, the planet attributed to the Tower card. Every battle has a winner and a loser; every Age has a constellation that rises at the Vernal Equinox and eventually passes away.

The Tower from *The Sacred Circle Tarot*

The bricks of the Tower are, in this context, the components of the Old Age: the arts, symbols, architecture, technology, societal structures, and leadership styles of the past. The metaphor can be extended to describe the mortar as the emotions, beliefs, and values that underpin the development of that age. When the bolt of lightning strikes the Tower, it heaves the bricks into the air; but in truth, it is the mortar that is most vulnerable to destruction. Mortar runs like a copper wire throughout the Tower's structure, conducting the blast of lightning from foundation to the peak. The components of the mortar, the beliefs and taboos, no longer function as a coherent bond between the bricks. When lightning strikes, the mortar is the first to come loose, and then the bricks fly.

Opening a portal to a new Aeon is not a solo act. One god alone can't shift an age. The process of opening and closing portals is wildly dramatic, showcasing characters of sizzling intensity and determination. Ancient peoples understood the need to dramatize the relationship between the overthrow of gods and the overthrow of cultures. In our times, Tolkien portrayed the end of an age as a Tower of evil that was undone when the Ring of Power was cast into the Crack of Doom. Aragorn, the new king, led the way into a new age, while the elves and other creatures of the old age passed into obscurity.

Tolkien, a notable scholar of ancient languages and texts, closely mimicked the motifs of the tales of Gilgamesh, Väinämöinen, Odin, Odysseus, Jason, Zeus, and Jamshid. But the old stories are fundamentally entwined with and make creative use of the three sciences of the ancients: numbers, music, and astronomy. Modern culture has plenty of poetry, and neo-mythologists like Tolkien, but their work is utterly detached from science rather than a metaphorical allegory for it. The shift from the Age of Pisces to the Age of Aquarius may be reduced to $E = mc^2$. The clash of force and power contained in Einstein's equation is very real, but it has a serious lack of personality and dramatic charm. The splitting of the atom unleashed the dogs of war in ancient terms, but without poetry, justice, or nobility. The bombing of Hiroshima makes for poor storytelling around a campfire.

Humans are caught between the clash of the gods and the terrors of the underworld, and are ground like dust between two stones. Human souls, in Plato's philosophy, are made of stardust, and return to dust, so the gods can build palaces on the mountain tops with the fresh meat of a new civilization. The people build temples to the new gods that reflect the beliefs of the new Aeon. The gods are the bricks of the people; the people are the bricks of the gods. The gods are the planets and stars; the people are star children.

Plato's view of the universe posited that time was well-ordered and regulated, a cyclic spiral measured by the revolving heavens. Space and its contents called forth the disorder and confusion that led to the downfall of the passing Aeon. The ending gasps of our Piscean Age have imposed technology on nature and the vast ocean of space, and conformed populations so they become unwitting slaves to linear time. The term "24/7/365" conveys the relentless dash for existence. Some cities never sleep. The agrarian cycles of seeding, growth, and harvest followed by winter rest are sublimated in the aisles of the local grocery store. Our mortar is failing.

The burgeoning of science and technology, while making lives easier in one sense, is numbing to the soul. Dumbed-down, drive-through spirituality is devoid of any relationship to the Earth and stars. Once severed from the skies and the seasons, it becomes easier to disregard the condition of the Earth and her ravaged landscape. Around-the-clock work schedules steal the soil of collective dreamtime. The very gods that merited promotion at the dawn of the age are failing to provide a moral compass for the use of dangerous technologies and international relationships. The revival of

Paganism and ethnic tribal religions reflect the longing for the return of cyclic time and a relationship with natural phenomena, but in practice they remain detached and unaware of the very astronomical data that gave names and life to the gods worshipped.

The Age of Pisces isn't over. The Tower is eroding, but it is still standing. The optimistic impulse to embrace the Age of Aquarius betrays a lack of awareness of the cataclysmic violence that historically attends the ending of a World Age. Of the many deck designs and designers, Crowley seems to have the best esoteric grasp of the realities of an Aeon shift. He even renamed the twentieth card "Aeon"; the old god fades into the background, and a divine child shimmers in the foreground. Lady Frieda's rendering of "The Tower" features a bolt of lightning emanating from a god's eye—the upheaval comes from a source in the heavens. Crowley knew very well what he was doing.

Astronomers are redefining the solar system. The elite cast of the sky gods, the planets, are being recast and supplemented. Pluto hovers over the galactic center, the star nursery at the heart of the Milky Way, teasing us with the spectre of global death, rebirth, and transformation from his seat at the far limits of our solar system. Gods are being created, killed, and reclassified with blithe abandon. Yet these archetypal characters are entwined with the fate of life on Earth through humanity's poetic consciousness of the changing Aeon.

We live in the time of the Tower, the passing of a World Age. It is a long, drawn-out process, and will not be finished in our lifetimes; it may not be completed for generations to come. The Age of Pisces erodes and fails, but the new gods are still gestating in the cosmic consciousness. The capacity for destruction has been expanded well beyond the scope of previous ages. The forces of nature (what nature does to people), the forces of war and conquest (what people do to other people), and the forces of species excess (what people do to nature) are all in play as the Age of Pisces ends. And may the gods help the poor fools hanging onto the bricks of the old Age when the Tower finally blows: they'll just help gravity do its job.

The Tower
Demolition

The Tower from *The Quest Tarot*

◆
✳
◆

The fierce awakening heralded by a trumpet's call will not be sounded until the rising Sun on Spring Equinox coincides with the stars of Aquarius, and that will take a few hundred more years. What are the bricks from the Age of Pisces that will be salvaged? Who will portray the gods that open the new portals in the sky? And will a cataclysmic war of the gods grind millions of people into dust in the process, or will we do it to ourselves?

There are no answers to these questions, but one thing is certain: those who love Mother Earth, the stars, and the waxing and ebbing of the Moon will always be closest to the gods who enact the shift, and are most likely to preserve and share the legends that never end.

Tarot and the Tree of Life

by Mary K. Greer

Both the Kabbalistic Tree of Life and tarot have big learning curves involving specialized terminology, organizing principles, correspondences and meanings. This article presents my favorite practical use of the Tree and tarot.

The Tree of Life, an important symbol in most cultures, is used in tarot practice as a Kabbalistic arrangement of ten spheres, called *sephiroth* (*sephira*, sing.), and the connecting paths among them, forming a mystical map of creation. First described in a Hebrew book called the *Sefer Yetzirah* (Book of Formation), Kabbalah began as a body of Jewish mystical principles encoded in the Hebrew alphabet and mapped on this Tree. Eventually, via adaptations by Christian mystics, it came to form the cornerstone and focus of the Western Esoteric Tradition. The tarot's Minor Arcana correspond to the ten sephiroth, which are considered containers, emanations, or attributes of God that constitute the revealed aspect of the divine. The Major Arcana correspond to the twenty-two paths between the sephiroth. Meditational practices called "climbing the Tree" purport to return the seeker to unity with divinity. When you descend the Tree you move into manifestation in the physical world.

With only a brief introduction to the sephiroth, you can use them to identify the major stages of any project. This moves you from the most abstract or ethereal stage of the creative process down to a concrete, mundane result. The tarot will then help you see where you are, so you can consider where you've come from, rethink the preceding steps if necessary, and plan your next step. Because of the flexibility of this system, you can examine your process at its broadest level and then use new Tree diagrams to plot specific views of any stage of the process.

To begin, determine a particular creative project in which you are involved. This can include such things as finding a job, writing a book, designing a garden, teaching a class, managing a team, starting a business, or planning a ritual.

Read through the descriptions of each sephira, starting with the most abstract urge to create something and stepping down through the various stages to the actual completed product. Name the stage and activities of your process that seem to go best with each sephira (astrological associations may be helpful to those familiar with them). Don't worry about defining things perfectly, as you should keep refining your diagram as you learn more. After doing this, you'll discover how to determine exactly where you are in the creative process and the specific activities on which to focus next.

Although we'll be moving from the first to the tenth sephira, you can as easily start by describing the final result (tenth sephira) and working your way back up to its initial starting place. Or, describe any known stage and work outward. I recommend drawing a blank Tree of Life diagram on a large sheet of paper (or multiple sheets taped together) and writing the stages of your creative project directly on this drawing.

One more thing: the Tree has three pillars (see diagram), each with its own qualities. The left and right pillars represent extremes. The left pillar is characterized by severity, form, or limitation; the right pillar represents mercy, force, or expansion. They must each be balanced by the activities and characteristics of the sephira opposite them (for instance, Chesed and Geburah need to balance each other) or be integrated by a sephira on the central pillar above or below them.

First Sephira—*Kether*
Middle pillar; attributed to the First Swirlings.
Crown. The alpha and omega. The place of beginnings. The urge to create. Your highest ideal. The spiritual source or reason for your project. The most abstract principles underlying the concept. Unity.

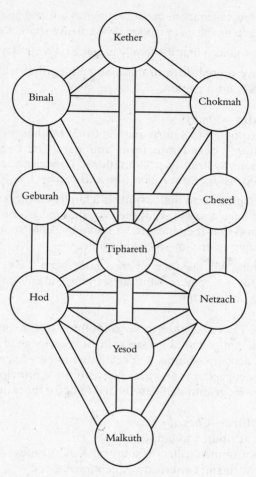

The Tree of Life

Examples:

1. The urge to get out in the fresh air and bond with others.
2. The urge to be comfortable when eating, working, relaxing.

Second Sephira—*Chokmah*
Right pillar; attributed to the zodiac and the Great Father.
The assertive will to create. The dynamic thrust and drive of spiritual

✦
✳
✦

life force energy. Inspiration. Initiative. Innovation. The first projection of an idea that puts things in motion. The creative spark. Revelation.

1. Dad announces that the family is going on a Sunday drive.

2. You have a great idea to make something that will physically support a person.

Third Sephira—*Binah*
Left pillar; attributed to Saturn and the Great Mother.
Understanding. Locked into form and patterns. Organization. Discrimination. Restrictions. Limitations. Concentration. Travail. Sorrow. Compassion. Conception (the idea "takes").

1. Mom reminds Dad that, as this is a family outing, everyone should have a say in what they do, that there'll be no junk food, and that they have to be home by 5 pm so as not to get caught in end-of-weekend traffic.

2. This thing will distance an erect body from the cold, hard floor but not require lying or standing. It will only serve one person at a time.

So far we have the urge to do something, an inspiration that excites, some limits, but not necessarily a knowledge of the specifics that will accomplish this. A special, unnumbered sephira called *Daath*, Knowledge, forms an abyss between these principles and the specific knowledge and abilities needed to carry them out below.

Fourth Sephira—*Chesed*
Right pillar; attributed to Jupiter.
Mercy. Opportunities. Gifts. Resources. Aids. Virtues. Abundance. Expansion. Altruism. Generosity. Acceptance. Good will. Beneficient rulership. Conformity. Loving kindness. Compassion. Gratitude.

1. Everyone shouts out all the places they want to go, and the friends and pets they want to bring with them, and about how much fun they'll have.

2. This thing needs to be strong, and soft, and luxurious, and elegant. The body must be well-supported—powerfully, flexibly, and at ease—with a pillowed seat and something to hold the back, arms, and legs.

Fifth Sephira—*Geburah*

Left pillar; attributed to Mars.

Severity. Challenges. Conflict. Readjustment. Endurance. Critical judgment, assessment and correction. Competiveness. Anger. Fear. Applied justice. Discipline. Destruction. Definition. Contraction. Self-assertion. Personal will, power, self-control.

1. The car only has five seatbelts: for the four in the family plus one, and since Trevor brought a friend last time, it's Sarah's turn. (Argue and no one goes!) As it's threatening rain, the beach and park are out, and they'll have to stop first for gas.

2. This thing needs extensions to keep one off the floor but not so high as to cause fear of falling. The back, arms, and pillow aren't really essential. Materials need to be available, sturdy, and workable with the tools at hand—for instance, wood, plastic, or metal. It needs to be done better and quicker than Joe's project, which is something similar.

Sixth Sephira—*Tiphareth*

Middle pillar; attributed to the Sun.

Beauty. Harmony. Conciliation. Mediation that balances and integrates all other sephiroth. Self-awareness. Identity. Individuality. Heart of the issue. Central goal or purpose. Healing. Death and rebirth; regeneration. Ability to sacrifice for one's ideals. Success. Blessing.

1. This is to be a "family outing" of quality time and mutual enjoyment. Each person has to be willing to give up a personal want so the family can experience an event together.

2. This thing for sitting on will be called a "chair." It will securely support a person in a seated position, between the above and below. Ideally, it will sacrifice luxury for comfort, and will balance beauty with practicality, utilizing materials that provide all of the above.

Seventh Sephira—*Netzach*

Right pillar; attributed to Venus.

Victory. Achievement of perfection in form and force and over false ideals. Emotional likes and dislikes. Attraction. Desire. Feelings. Aesthetic and sensual pleasure. Appreciation. Enjoyment. All forms of relationship polarities. Mystery. Magic. Glamour. The arts. Firmness. Valor (steadfastly facing emotional difficulties).

1. Each person names five things he'd get the most pleasure from doing and two that he wouldn't like. If attracted by something in another's list, he can add that item.

2. Here go all the considerations about what will make this chair attractive and desirable: the aesthetics of the materials, the shape, and the sensual experience of the fit so that a person wants to sit in it. (From an advertising point of view—what would make the public desire one?)

Eighth Sephira—*Hod*
Left pillar; attributed to Mercury.
Splendor (of the illuminated or light-filled mind). Thoughts. Concrete mind and intellect. Reason. Ethics. Diligence. Restraint. Mental representations. Metaphors. Symbolic and magical forms. Communication. Imparting, exchanging, connecting information. Craft. Skill. Wit. Science. Technology. Plans and diagrams.

1. The elements of each desired activity are evaluated in terms of the time, distance, weather, family quality, and number of people interested. Rain nixes the outdoors. A movie doesn't involve family sharing. Museums are boring. They might consult a map, tourism book, or the Internet.

2. Here go the patterns, measurements, drawings, descriptions. What will make it straight, level, and proportional? What skills and tools are needed to produce this chair?

Ninth Sephira—*Yesod*
Middle pillar; attributed to the Moon.
Foundation. Mood and atmosphere drawing on the astral and etheric planes. Inherited karma and DNA—what is brought from the past, plus the unconscious longing or urge toward future union. Habits and conditioning. Reactive emotions. Suppressed and repressed material. Procreative and survival drives. Sexuality. Vital life energy. Fertility. Dreams, vision, psychism. Growth, fluctuation, tides. Images. Fantasy. The integration of mind and emotions.

1. Family history suggests they will wrangle until it's too late to go anywhere. Repressed family dynamics start to take over. Trevor fantasizes about throwing his sister off a cliff, Mom longs to get away to the gym, Dad envisions roping them all together, Sarah feels like she's falling into a raging sea, when suddenly her friend suggests they go indoor

rock climbing. The image captures all their imaginations and the tide turns.

2. Envisioning the chair in all its details before it's built (constructing it on the astral) generates energy to move forward. The chair is conceptualized as the next evolutionary leap, creating previously unforeseen possibilities. A whole factory for chairs is imagined.

Tenth Sephira—*Malkuth*
Middle pillar; attributed to the Earth.
Kingdom. Sensory life of the physical world. The supreme manifestation of the form conceived in the initial triad. The end result. Grounding point for the creative powers of spirit ("as above, so below"). Nature. The body and all material existence.

1. The family arrives at the indoor climbing facility. They spend the next several hours climbing together, have a great time, and get home by 5 pm, tired but happy.

2. Someone makes the chair and sits in it.

The Next Step
As if this delineation of your creative process wasn't informative enough, the next phase is even more enlightening. Separate the Major Arcana from your tarot deck. Shuffle the Majors only and pick one at random while asking, "In regards to this project, what creative force or energy is wanting to work through me right now?" Find that card among the paths on the Tree of Life diagram. It will show a path between two sephiroth, illustrating the move from one stage to another. Interpretation of your Major Arcana card will tell you the kind of energy that's striving to express itself in the next stage. The sephira from which it descends will tell you where that energy comes from, and the sephira it's moving toward tells you what tasks are needed to actualize the coming stage. Then find the Minor Arcana number cards associated with the higher numbered sephira (toward which you are moving).

For instance, the Tower is on the path moving from the seventh sephira, Netzach, to the eighth sephira, Hod (from the sensual and emotional stage to the rational). The four eights in the Minor Arcana correspond to Hod. The energy you are working with (the Tower) is explosive and seemingly destructive. It represents the wrenching apart of mind and emotions, the anger and conflict that arise when flaws in one are lit up by insight from the other. The Tower also

◆ allows for the project to be broken down into smaller units that can
✳ be evaluated rationally and put into a now-flawless plan or design.
◆ Note that it's possible to seemingly skip a stage (from sephira six to
nine, for instance). In fact, during any major creative process you'll constantly be revisiting earlier stages and exploring new ones in a cyclic manner.

Now, examine the corresponding Minor Arcana cards associated with the sephira you are moving toward. They will indicate specific tasks that you need to address at this stage/sephira. In the example, these would be the Eight of Wands, Cups, Swords, and Pentacles. Rather than interpreting them according to book meanings, play with possible associations they may have to this stage of your project. The suit cards are the brainstorming tools of fire, water, air, and earth that suggest new possibilities and directions for you to take. Brainstorming possibilities with a friend might help you generate more options. Be playful. Give free reign to your imagination.

If you wish, identify specific ideas or activities indicated by the Minor Arcana cards associated with the sephira at the lower end of the path. The Major Arcana card shows the energy that is moving you from one to the other. In terms of the Tree as a whole, note how vitally important the sixth sephira Tiphareth is, being directly linked to every other stage except the final one. It emphasizes the principle that you must constantly work at getting to the real heart of your project.

It is the addition of tarot that makes this such a powerful activity, fostering growth in new and productive directions, guided by deep insight into a broad, linked overview of the whole process that your Tree outline depicts. Using the Tree in your daily life attunes you to cosmic, divine emanations at work in everything, and familiarizes you with the real-world dimensions of the landscape traveled in magical pathworking.

Voicing Blessings

by Janina Renée

When we are working with tarot cards that portray certain types of characters, one way we can integrate these cards' meanings while activating their good energies is to bless the people they represent. For example, the appearance of the Empress suggests a range of issues involving one's own mother as well as mother archetypes, so upon drawing this card (or any time you feel like it), you can say something like:

> I bless my mother,
> and wish her all of the love and abundance
>   that the Empress freely bestows.
> I bless the Great Mother
>   whose image I see in the life of the universe:
>   in Heaven, in Earth, and within me.
> So may I also receive the blessing of the Empress,
>   the blessing of the Mother,
> that I may nurture beauty and loving kindness,
>   for myself and for all the world.

Indeed, in keeping with the last sentiment, any expression of loving kindness, including loving kindness meditations, also express the Empress qualities.

As a tarot rite to surround your mother with good energies, you could lay out the Sun, the Empress, and the World on an altar space, along with candles, crystals, and flowers.

You can perform similar blessings when you draw the Emperor, which often stands for your own father or other father figures. This can activate the powerful qualities of the Emperor archetype within you, and help you connect with the ideal of the Sacred King as manifested in the earthly king. You could say something like,

> I bless my father,
> and wish him all of the strength and respect
>   that the Emperor embodies.
> I bless the Great Father
>   whose workings I see
>   in the ordering principles of the universe.
> So may I also receive the blessing of the Emperor,
>   the blessing of the Father,
> that I may work for the betterment
>   of myself and of all the world.

To activate the Great Father/Emperor within, apply logic and order to your own world, starting with your character, home, and mode of work.

Of course, blessings don't need to be long and involved. "Light Workers," who are people who are working to make the world a better place, can be represented by the Star card, so with the appearance of the Star, you could say, "May all Light Workers be blessed with light-heartedness and success." This is also something you might do whenever you see the morning or evening star (the planet Venus). When you draw the Lovers, or when you see a couple in love, you could say, "May all lovers enjoy continued happiness."

With the varied cast of characters who appear in the tarot deck, many other blessing occasions will suggest themselves.

Metaphysical Tarot

by Leeda Alleyn Pacotti

I n Western culture, we are taught to look forward and outward. We become accustomed to perceiving our problems in external circumstances and relationships. Even when we know a problem has its basis in an inner construct, we still look outside ourselves, placing blame on this person, that event, or those conspiring circumstances. In short, we project.

Projection is an attendant, normal trait of the human mind. If not for the ability to project, we would never choose a certain home or desire a particular vehicle. We wouldn't rise to challenges, because we would not imagine an outcome of victory—or any outcome at all. A refined ability of projection, or an imaginative thought, orders the priorities in our lives and defines the steps we take toward achievement. The natural ability of projection is the connection between "I want it" and "I got it."

When we misuse projection (which is often the case), we don't want to recognize that our problems arise from what we believe, think, or feel. Anger from others comes for no reason, and we are simply unwitting targets. Confusion about answers on forms or missed traffic directions happen all by themselves, and we have to straighten them out. Faced with continual roadblocks, we can't understand why our way is continually thwarted.

The human mind is very powerful, containing both conscious and subconscious mechanisms. When we refuse to deal with our anger, confusion, frustration, or any other emotion that inhibits our progress toward fulfillment and happiness, the subconscious creates situations, relationships, and displays to show us how we are doing. If our consciously held premises are wrong, we will encounter people, books, or events that highlight the falsities of our beliefs or theories.

How Tarot Divination Helps

The images of tarot unveil clues about the basis of our inner turmoil and insubstantial thinking. As long as the tarot reader has taken in the particular symbols of a tarot deck, it becomes easy to apprehend the forces of awareness.

Each Major Arcana card in tarot directly evokes a primary state of mind, which is reinforced in other Major cards and throughout the Minor Arcana. When the Major Arcana cards are upright in any tarot spread, they exemplify the nobler face of an awareness; when they are reversed, the opposite attitude is predominant. When an awareness is beginning to surface, it seems indefinable. To focus in on this awareness, we must understand that its mental framework is subtle and elusive, but prevalent and pervasive—such as an underlying negative attitude that something will always go wrong, or a pervasive positive one that everything works out for the best.

The states of conscious awareness, symbolized in the Major Arcana, have distinct polarities:

The Fool: Open-mindedness/Rigidity

The Magician: Attention/Distraction

The High Priestess: Remembrance/Forgetfulness

The Empress: Imagination/Dullness

The Emperor: Reason/Irrationality

The Hierophant: Knowledge/Ignorance

The Lovers: Equality/Difference

The Chariot: Mastery/Inability

Strength: Courage/Fear

The Hermit: Unity/Scatteredness

The Wheel of Fortune: Expansiveness/Narrowness

Justice: Fairness/Prejudice

The Hanged Man: Interdependence/Isolation

Death: Fertility/Sterility

Temperance: Moderation/Uncontrollability

The Devil: Error/Delusion

The Tower: Deconstruction/Destruction

The Star: Meditation/Thoughtlessness

The Moon: Organization/Disarray

The Sun: Regeneration/Deterioration

Judgement: Commitment/Vacillation

The World: Universality/Materiality

Although these terms describing the states of consciousness seem definitive, other descriptive words will be appropriate when the consciousness is first apprehended, while it develops, and later as it flowers.

What tarot provides us is a milestone of our spiritual maturation. Many individuals will work to bring forward or develop one state of consciousness in a lifetime. Depending on how willing they are to recognize and utilize that consciousness, they may spend one or more other lifetimes integrating that awareness into their broadening personalities.

In contrast, other people may have lifetimes of spiritual challenges, which a variety of tarot Arcana reveal. Taken at different

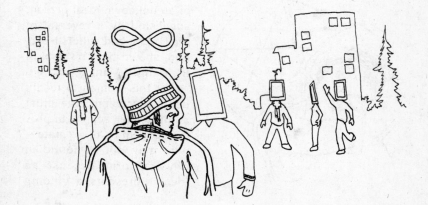

points in life, the symbolism will show a combination of mental forces exerting extreme pressure to hasten a delayed maturity. These individuals have lifetimes full of unusual events outside the accepted norm, and seem to make inexplicable decisions that have a protracted series of unanticipated consequences. Appearances do deceive! Often the most chaotic and turbulent of lives is the red flag of rapid spiritual progression, although it may seem frivolous and unsubstantiated.

Making the Most of Life's Drama

First and foremost, own your thoughts and attitudes. From the Source of All, you have been given attributes, talents, and ideas specific to your spiritual evolution and your strengthening character.

Why does the life mission go awry? We live in a world of human interaction, where we are taught not to ask probing questions but rather to guess at intents. In learning not to question others deeply, we also fail to question ourselves. When we forfeit inner communication of our personal symbolism, projection takes over, attracting to us examples of the problems we are to solve.

A person who loves passionately and is willing to make a commitment becomes surprised at the hatefulness expressed by family, friends, and coworkers to her ideas. Gradually, she feels isolated and adrift. The more she suffers rejection, the more she sorrows over her failure to find love.

Were the person in this scenario to seek a tarot reading, she might find the Major Arcana cards of the Fool, the Lovers, the Hanged Man, and Judgement. From the Fool and Judgement, she has the capacities of commitment and open-mindedness. However,

she harbors a secret image of an unknown ideal person, suggested by a reversal of the Lovers, and suffers isolation, shown by a reversal of the Hanged Man.

For this woman to rectify her life problem, she must admit to her secret, unprofessed ideal of a love mate—who may not be found in physical form. Because an ideal represents a guiding aspiration, she is unwittingly letting everyone else know that they don't measure up.

The exasperation of others with her attitudes results in ostracism, leaving this woman alone and in pain. Acknowledging interaction and interdependence on everyone else, this woman needs to release dependence on the outer world and, like the Hanged Man, regain faith in the plan laid out for her life. By letting go of the consuming search for the ideal man, she can begin to rebuild relationships in all parts of her life. Restructuring her search for perfection in another allows her to create and manifest the developments of perfection and completion within herself—by nurturing and maturing her role in interactions with others.

Digesting a Tarot Apple-a-Day

Although a full tarot spread gives a well-rounded picture of the disarray of or command over the motive forces of your consciousness, consider drawing one tarot card each evening, while relaxing after work. Either the full deck or the Major Arcana alone can be used. Leave the card upright or reversed as it was drawn from the deck. Now, study the symbolism of the card.

As you gain proficiency with the symbols, you form a personal recognition of how they attach to specific types of people, conversations, attitudes, and events that entered into or imposed on the day. If the card is reversed, your consciousness expressed a negativity, upset, and rejection toward the day's experiences. If the card is upright, you have exhibited positivity, poise, and acceptance.

While still viewing the card, consider what you did well and how you can build upon the ability. If your attitude was toward the negative, be objective about the upsetting situations and fair in your assessment of your developing consciousness. After all, did you really know how to be better at that given moment? If you incorporate your observations into a meditation or as a dream question before sleeping, your subconscious mind will elaborate on strengthening or correcting your ability and your conscious control of it.

Life is referred to as an experience, because you are here to test yourself and gain knowledge. The circumstances and people around you are mirrors of your true nature within. Like the changing expressions you have from day to day, so these reflections change, too. Dare to alter your inner landscape to the noblest character. Be open, genuine, courageous, fair, and kind.

♦ None of us is truly alone, even in moments of despair or difficulty.
✳ By all means, be pleased with every person, thought, and event for
♦ showing you who you are and helping you seek ways to change your
182 life for the better. Your soul light will shine all the brighter.

Seeking the Gods

by Rachel Pollack

There are many ways to approach the tarot, and almost as many ways to approach a tarot reading. At one extreme, perhaps, are the people who steadfastly refuse to learn anything of the cards' symbolism or meanings. They prefer to seek inspiration directly from the cards and the moment. Sometimes that inspiration is psychic, a perception of knowledge and secrets. I look at, say, the Eight of Wands, and the name Fred comes to mind, and a red Volkswagen, and a trip to Boston where a yellow and black cat on a street corner leads to a discovery of love. Sometimes the inspiration is psychological or poetic. I look at the Eight of Wands and I feel the complexity of someone's life, the danger of everything catching up with him all at once.

Direct inspiration is one extreme; the other is memorization of meanings. You turn over a card and you bring to mind the exact list of "divinatory meanings" given in your favorite tarot book or the LWB (the little white booklet that comes with every deck). I know a tarot teacher who will not allow his students to do any readings until they have memorized all 156 meanings for the cards (seventy-eight upright and seventy-eight reversed). Otherwise, he says, they might make mistakes. Such an idea startles the direct imagination group, for to them the meaning of the card lies in the moment, and in the encounter between the reader, the querent, the question, and the picture. For my friend, however, and many others, the meanings of the cards are not arbitrary or random. They belong to a complex system that involves numbers, astrological correspondences, elemental energies, and many other factors. The pictures are not whimsical but meant to convey specific information.

There is a problem with this approach. If you want to use the intended meanings for the cards, whose meanings do you use? The designer of the specific deck? Or do you go back further and look at tarot tradition? And which tradition? The Kabbalist and astrological correspondences of the Golden Dawn and other "Hermetic" orders? Or the traditions of cartomancy—the lists of meanings that largely began with the eighteenth-century tarot reader and occultist Etteilla?

On the other hand, what outside concepts do we bring when we allow ourselves to improvise on the images? For the past quarter-century or so the improvisation has been mostly psychological. We look at the cards and ask ourselves (or the querent) how it feels, or about the attitude of the people in the pictures. Since this is very difficult to do when there are no people on the cards, we tend to avoid decks in the old Marseille tradition, where the suit cards do not show any scenes. Many assume that the pip cards contain no symbolism, that they are empty of meaning, simply because they are not psychological. There actually is quite a bit of symbolic imagery in the Marseille cards—they just are not about states of mind.

The psychological approach to tarot is very valuable, and I have followed it for many years. Recently, however, I have been looking more and more for ways to go beyond it (see my article in Llewellyn's *2007 Tarot Reader*, "Toward a New Tarot"). We could, of course, go back to those systems of "official" meanings. But suppose we want to add something new?

One way to open up the tarot to something beyond psychology is to look at what Goddes are present in the cards (I use "Goddes" to represent the whole array of gods and goddesses). You do not have to believe in the objective reality of myth to find this meaningful. The Goddes do not have to be real the way your dentist is real, or the

The Two of Cups from The Universal Tarot of Marseille

washing machine is real. Think of the Goddes as concentrations of energy, or ways in which a formless divine manifests itself. Or think of them as deep and potent stories.

Of course, you may very well experience the Goddes in the same way you experience your dentist. I know a woman who talks regularly with the Egyptian god Thoth, by legend the creator of the tarot. The Greek god Hermes now and then plays tricks on me (some people consider Thoth and Hermes to be the same being; I prefer to think of them as cousins). The goddess Artemis once took the form of a goat to rescue my partner and me when we were lost in a dense fog on a mountaintop with sheer drops on either side. But that's me; I don't expect other people to seek such personal encounters.

What matters, I think, is that the Goddes have personality and character; they have powerful stories and qualities. They are not vague, or formless, each one just like the other. To see what Godde is present, or active, in a card or a reading is to recognize a particular power and its effects on our lives.

There are things we can do when we identify the Godde that is present. We may create talismans, or magic formulas, or sigils to honor and invoke their power. We might wear their colors or metals (copper for Isis, gold for Aphrodite), or eat their foods (barley for Osiris or Demeter, pomegranates for Persephone or Dionysius). In this way we can bring the reading alive, make it physical and not simply a discussion. Perhaps the most potent action is to retell the myths and see how our own lives fit into these large and ancient tales. Once we identify a card as Isis, or Hermes, and that card comes up in a reading, we can recall their stories and see what that means in the moment of the reading.

The question is, how do we identify them? If indeed there are major differences between say, Zeus and Dionysius, or Aphrodite and Athena, how do we know which ones are invoked in any card? (I am using primarily the Greek deities because they are the ones I experience most strongly; the same principles should apply to other pantheons, such as the Egyptian Neteru or the African Orishas.)

In the Major Arcana we already know many mythological connections for the twenty-two cards. The Magician is often identified as Hermes or Thoth, the High Priestess is seen as Egyptian Isis or Greek Persephone, the Empress is identified with both Aphrodite (love) and Demeter (motherhood), the Emperor with Zeus, and so on.

But where are the Goddes in the Minor Arcana? How do we identify a divine presence for these cards of daily life? The Court Cards are easy, for many deck creators have specifically named them as deities. In the *Daughter of the Moon* tarot each Court Card is a specific goddess, drawn from many cultures. The *Haindl Tarot* uses the deities of four specific cultures, one for each suit, to identify its "Mother, Father, Daughter, Son" cards.

Ah, but the numbered cards. Their traditions carry much less identification with mythic figures. Even the *Mythic Tarot* (dedicated to Greek mythology) and the various Celtic or Egyptian decks do not relate the Minor cards to individual gods or goddesses.

One way to identify Goddes in these cards is through the Kabbalah Tree of Life. There are ten places, called sephiroth (singular, sephirah) on the Tree, and each one belongs to various deities grouped around the theme of that sephirah. Position Three, for example, called Binah, or Understanding, evokes the Great Mother figures, while Six—Tipheret, or Beauty—goes with dying and resurrecting gods, from Christ to Greek Dionysius to Norse Balder.

One problem with this system is that it does not distinguish the numbers by suit. That is, all Threes belong to Binah, all Sixes to Tipheret. Which dying and resurrecting god would be specifically the Three of Wands as compared to the Three of Cups, or Swords, or Pentacles? Perhaps we can just choose which one seems appropriate. As a figure of glorious light, Balder might be the Six of Wands (Wands usually is associated with fire). Dionysius, the god of wine, could be the Six of Cups. Should Christ be the Six of Swords, due to the painfulness of his death? And which dying and resurrecting god might be the Six of Pentacles?

In the Golden Dawn system, the Two through Ten of each suit refer to specific "decans," that is, ten degrees of the zodiac. (Nine cards in each suit multiplied by four suits equals thirty-six cards, and the zodiac, like all circles, is divided into 360 degrees; the Aces for each suit stand apart, as representations of the pure element for that suit.) So for example, the Two of Wands signifies Mars in Aries, the Three of Wands is the Sun in Aries, and the Four of Wands represents Venus in Aries. Since the planets are all related to gods (Mars is the god of war; the Sun is Apollo, god of art and prophecy; Venus is the goddess of love) we can use these astrological designations to determine the Goddes for Two through Ten of each suit.

I would like to suggest a slightly different approach to identifying cards with specific deities. Each of the forty numbered cards carries a certain tradition of cartomantic meanings. Why not use these meanings, combined with the modern tradition of imagery (derived primarily from the *Rider-Waite-Smith* tarot) to see what deities emerge in our own work with the cards?

Clearly this is a subjective choice rather than a system. But aren't all systems simply a collection of choices? Rather than providing a list of associations that would just be the way I see the possibilities, I will give a couple of examples. Hopefully this will demonstrate what I mean, so that others can make their own decisions.

As mentioned above, much of the tradition of meanings derives from the work of Etteilla in the eighteenth century. Here is what he says about the Three of Wands:

> Enterprise, to undertake, to commence, to encroach, to take possession of, audacity, temerity, boldness, imprudence, enterprising, bold, rash, audacious, undertaken, encumbered, disconcerted, crippled, effort, try, temptation. *Reversed:* Interruption of misfortunes, of torments, of suffering, of travail, end, cessation, discontinuation, discontinuance, repose, influence, intermediary, intermission.

If we see the main qualities here as enterprising, bold, audacious, what forceful Goddes might we find in this energy? There are hero figures, such as Hercules or some of the warrior goddesses (Babylonian Ishtar, for example). My own choice might be Apollo, for even though he emphasizes light and beauty, he also is very bold, the light conquering the dark. There are negative sides to this god: overconfidence, arrogance, the masculine set against the feminine. But who said the Goddes for each card had to be completely admirable? One of the interesting qualities of polytheism is that we get to look at the less desirable sides of the divine energy.

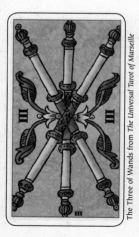

The Three of Wands from *The Universal Tarot of Marseille*

The Three of Wands from *The Universal Tarot*

The Three of Trees from *The Shining Tribe Tarot*

We also need to consider if the *Rider-Waite-Smith* picture illustrates the qualities described by Etteilla and those who followed him. Is the man standing on the hilltop bold and audacious and enterprising? Many people think of him as enigmatic, not really knowing just what to make of him standing there with his back to us (interesting that no one has ever suggested he might be rude!). If we think of him as Apollo looking out over the world (or a masculine version of Ishtar) it might give us a better way to understand the card.

Consider also the Four of Wands. Etteilla says about this card:

Society, association, assembly, liaison, federation, alliance, assembly, reunion, circle, community, mob, multitude, crowd, rout, crew, band, company, cohort, army, convocation, accompaniment, mixture, medley, allow, amalgam, covenant, convention, pact, treaty. *Reversed:* Prosperity, augmentation, increase, advancement, success, thriving, good luck, flourishing, happiness, beauty, embellishment.

The emphasis here on community, whether for good or bad, could suggest Goddes whose main quality is to safeguard society and communal life. Among the Greeks, this suggests Athena, who often was depicted as dedicated to the good of her city, Athens. According to myth, both she and Poseidon applied for the job of protecting the young city-state. Poseidon offered horses—animals used primarily for war and conquest. Athena offered the olive

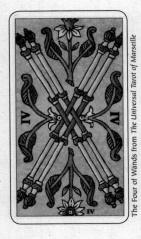

The Four of Wands from *The Universal Tarot of Marseille*

The Four of Wands from *The Universal Tarot*

The Four of Trees from *The Shining Tribe Tarot*

tree—for nourishment and commerce. The wise Athenians chose the wonderful olive, symbol of stability and wisdom as well as good food, for an olive tree can live for thousands of years. Besides, Athena was a powerful warrior when that was necessary.

Waite's meanings for this card shift the energy slightly:

> Country life, haven of refuge, harvest home, repose, concord, harmony, prosperity, peace, the perfected work of these, unexpected good fortune. *Reversed:* The meaning remains unaltered, prosperity, increase, felicity, beauty, embellishment. A married woman will have beautiful children.

Athena still can be found in these meanings, for even though she was a warrior she first of all sought concord and harmony in the community. However, the emphasis here on country life, and the prosperous home, suggests more intimate Goddes, less concerned with the larger society. One possibility among the Greeks would be Hestia, goddess of the hearth. Since the suit is Wands, and the element of fire, the Irish goddess Bridget, keeper of the eternal flame, would be another example.

These are just two cards, and many, I am sure, will disagree with my choices (I can hear the voices now—"She thinks *Athena* is the Four of Wands? Is she crazy?"). Again, I do not offer them as definitive, and certainly not objective. Instead, I hope they will demonstrate a fresh way of looking at the Minor Arcana.

Judgment

Deck Reviews

The Tarot of Mermaids

reviewed by Annie Jones

My initial attraction to the *Tarot of Mermaids* deck, by Pietro Alligo, was the notion of the mermaids themselves. I happen to really like mermaids. Okay, I admit that I've never actually met one, but there was always something about them that I found compelling. They were mysterious, yet approachable. They somehow seemed to know secrets that we were yet unaware of. I consider them graceful, intuitive beings—gentle yet strong, elusive and powerful. The inherent mystique of mermaids is a comfortable fit with the traditions of tarot. I feel the images presented here reinforced my conception and added to my curiosity.

I was actually unprepared for the amount of nudity present in the cards. At first I thought, "Enough already! How about an occasional shell bra or some other simple adornment, please!" But after all, they *are* mermaids, and as such are not known for their sense of couture. No starry-eyed, innocent little mermaids here! For anyone who feels uncomfortable or offended by topless female mer-people, this deck is certainly not for you. However, once over the distraction of the abundant nudity, these cards are absolutely gorgeous. Being an artist at heart, I feel the artwork by Mauro De Luca was done in a tasteful and sensitive manner. They are depicted as strong, beautiful females, and that isn't a bad thing.

XVIII
The Moon

La Luna
La Lune

La Luna
Der Mond

The Moon from Tarot of Mermaids

This is a standard seventy-eight–card deck, with obvious *Rider-Waite-Smith* influences. There are several areas where the deck deviates from the *RWS*, but the variations do not detract from the ability to read with and understand this deck for someone who is familiar with the *RWS*.

First, the deck is dominated by female figures (with the exception of the Kings, the Emperor, the Hierophant, the Hermit, and the driver of the Chariot). There are various other mermen depicted on some of the cards, in minor roles. However, the heart of the story certainly lies with the females.

The Court Cards consist of Kings, Queens, Knights, and Knaves. The Kings are portrayed as very masculine and decidedly older than the figures in most of the other cards. They project a sense of authority and wisdom. The Queens are infused with some basic *RWS* symbolism. Nothing new is necessarily added, except for the underwater surroundings. The Knights, now portrayed by women, evoke the same sense of strength and determination that the traditional male knights do, and for this particular deck I don't find the gender switch a problem. The Knaves, the equivalent of the Pages in the *RWS*, are all female, and appear young and curious. No surprises here.

Although the traditional names of each suit are printed on each card, the icons depicted in the minor arcana have been changed to represent the aquatic nature of this deck. In a nutshell (or should I say clamshell?), Wands are now Oars, Swords are a three-pronged Trident, Cups are Shells, and Pentacles are Pearls. The suits are all cast in suit-specific color schemes, enhancing the overall tone of each suit.

The fiery nature of the suit of Wands comes through with the use of warm, orangey-cream hues. Much, if not most, of the overall action on these cards takes place above the water (as is also true for the suit of Swords). I think this refers to the more human, intellectual side of the mermaids. The cards read with similar *RWS* correspondences, with a few exceptions. For example, the *RWS* Five of Wands has a rather negative, competitive feel, suggesting that the situation is one of discord. The mermaids in this Five of Wands depict a lighter, more playful rivalry, as if a group of young, frolicking girls are having a slumber party, engaging in their version of a pillow fight. I feel a more friendly opposition in this card, as if it's telling us we should lighten up.

The suit of Cups is displayed in subtle shades of blue and green, lending itself well to the underwater scenes. The colors also evoke a sense of emotional peace, even in the cards with a more somber tone. The waters all appear to be calm. There is nothing particularly unique or striking about this new twist on Cups, and I've found that these cards read as easily as any *RWS* variation.

Exploring the suit of Swords was most interesting. The mermaids and tritons depicted have snake-like tails instead of the traditional fin-tail. It makes these particular mer-people come across as more reptilian, giving them a more sinister, less approachable nature. The deep blue and purple hues add to the overall gloomy and threatening tone. Again, no huge surprises as far as how these cards translate, but one card I find particularly interesting is the Ten of Swords.

I see this mermaid as a whale that has chosen to beach herself on the shore. She is obviously exhausted and weak, and will probably not last long without help. I don't get the sense that she is dead. The tridents surrounding her are not impaling her body. The Ten of Swords in the *RWS* shows the swords piercing the body to the point of death—an exaggerated, dramatic, and final death. The mermaid version reads as though the situation is more self-inflicted, as opposed to some kind of outside force or influence having brought her here. It appears that she could carefully, but not easily, be removed from the confines of the tridents either by her own sheer will or with the proper assistance. The sky also appears to be clearing, indicating that the situation will at least not be worsened by the onset of a storm. The implication is that you have reached rock bottom—but also that perhaps

The Ten of Swords from *Tarot of Mermaids*

you brought it on yourself. It may not be easy to remedy this situation, but it is not completely without hope. A better day can still come.

Despite appearances, the last suit is Pearls, and not bubbles! Something about the large size, the translucent appearance, and the sensation of floating all scream *bubbles!* to me. I do like the underwater translation from coins to pearls, but the visual interpretations left me unimpressed. The red and teal colors give this suit an earthy, sensual feel. However, there is also a bit of a heavy, sluggish contrast between the heat of the reds and the placid teal. This is also the most androgynous of all the suits.

Finally, we come to the Major Arcana. The Fool's journey as told in the *Tarot of Mermaids* offers only subtle differences from our traditional understanding. I do have a few favorites, and a few areas where I feel the cards stray somewhat from our usual interpretations.

First, I need to talk about the Tower. Here we see two mermaids tumbling from atop a blazing lighthouse. However, they are falling back into the water! Is it just me, or is that not a bad thing if you are a mermaid? The waters may be turbulent, and maybe the fall is unexpected, but it's not catastrophic. Also, there is no indication of how the fire started. Maybe it was slow and smoldering, rather than sudden, as implied by the more typical lightning. These subtle changes slightly alter the implications for me.

Another favorite is the Star. We find this mermaid sitting on the shore, and it appears that her tailfin is transforming into two legs.

The Tower from *Tarot of Mermaids*

Isn't that the wish of every little mermaid? Do I hear a song coming on? I love this representation of a wish coming true. Also, the fact that the transition is not yet complete gives us the feeling of hopefulness. We could be witnessing a positive, life-changing event. Take a deep breath and give thanks!

The Strength card is very calm, and exudes a sense of patience paying off. It also reads as the fortitude to adapt to new and potentially challenging situations. This is illustrated by a mermaid depicted in an arid, desert-like area—who seems very serene and comfortable. Her hair has been swept into an elaborate infinity symbol and she appears very tranquil. The beast she is taming, in this case a large walrus, appears more docile and content than the typical lion of the *RWS*, illustrating self control.

The feminine energy of the Moon is enhanced here by the powerful symbol of the mermaids themselves. They are mysterious and elusive and add to the idea of illusion often associated with this card. The small crayfish is now a full grown mermaid with a crustacean tail, straining to pull herself on to land. Is this a creature to be feared? We feel attracted, yet at the same time cautious. She appears to be struggling, but is she? The LWB [Little White Book] refers to unpredictability and the unknown, as well as the attraction and mysteries of femininity. All are captured here in this unique depiction.

The LWB contains a short background on mermaids and their history as well as an eight-card spread in the shape of a mermaid. There are also brief keyword descriptions of each card in several languages. This deck is as functional as it is beautiful. Anyone looking for a flowing, engaging deck should explore the depths of the *Tarot of Mermaids*.

Tarot of the Thousand and One Nights

reviewed by Elizabeth Hazel

Occasionally the artwork of a particularly prolific or important older artist is recycled, and their work is recast into
the structure of a tarot deck. Sometimes this works, and
sometimes it doesn't. In the case of Lo Scarabeo's *Tarot of the
Thousand and One Nights*, featuring artwork by Leon Carré, the
combination offers a luminous addition to any deck collection.

Léon Georges Jean Baptiste Carré (1878–1942) was born in
Granville, France, and conducted a good part of his career in
Algeria. He exhibited in important art salons in Paris from 1900 until
1911. During this period, noteworthy "gift book" illustrators such
as Edmund Dulac and Arthur Rackham were reaching the peaks of
their careers because of the improvements in color-separation techniques in printing. Carré worked in watercolor, pastel, and oil medi-
ums, and did poster-art work for commercial products and travel
advertisements in his early career. His advertising posters were
typical for the time period, and did not involve the Asian-influenced
style that came to be known as "orientale." This artistic style, a
western fusion of Persian, Indian, and Chinese ornamentation, was
already established and popular, and was used to perfection Dulac's
illustrations for *The Arabian Nights* (Hodder and Staughton, 1907).
Twenty years later, Carré closely mimicked Dulac's techniques in his

THE DEVIL
EL DIABLO
XV
IL DIAVOLO
LE DIABLE

DER TEUFEL
DE DUIVEL

The Devil from *Tarot of the Thousand and One Nights*

pictures for the same literary work. At first glance, I thought that Dulac's work had been used for this deck. Carré's illustrations in the orientale idiom are similar to Dulac's, but of course, there are differences.

In the mid-1920s, Carré was commissioned to create illustrations for a twelve-volume edition of *Le Livre des Mille Nuits et Une Nuit*, published by L'Édition d'Art H. Piazza. Most other editions of *The Arabian Nights*, including the one illustrated by Dulac, were abridged and contained only the widely popular portions of this important collection of stories. From 1926 until 1932 (or 1936, as the sources differ), Carré produced almost one hundred illustrations for this series of books. His illustrations were framed with ornamentation by Racim Mohammed. Both drawings and ornamental frames are used in the tarot deck (although only Carré is credited).

The Tarot of the Thousand and One Nights is accompanied by a LWB [Little White Book] typical of Lo Scarabeo deck productions. A short history of *The Arabian Nights* is given as a preface, followed by keyword descriptions of the card meanings. Yet I was intensely curious to discover the characters and stories depicted in the illustrations. This led to a great deal of frustrating research. Not a single library on the North American continent owns the complete twelve-volume edition, although random volumes are scattered across the country. The Franklin Library (a book club) produced an abridged volume featuring a few of Carré's illustrations in 1978. And in 2006, a high-end "coffee-table book" publisher, Assouline, released another abridged edition of *The Arabian Nights*, featuring some (but nowhere near all) of Carré's drawings. The Assouline edition is a sumptuous luxury production, to be sure, but it features no more illustrations than the Franklin Edition (and at a much, much higher price). However, both the Franklin and Assouline editions include some of the artwork not chosen for the deck.

These two editions did give me a chance to compare a handful of the drawings selected for specific cards and their appropriateness for the cards' divinatory meanings. For example, the illustration used for the Devil card is captioned: "*His head was as a dome, his hands like pitchforks, his legs as long as masts and his mouth big as a cave.*" The picture is from the tale "The Fisherman and the Jinni." In this story, a fisherman pulls a brass jar out of the sea. When he opens it, he releases an Ifrit (a jinni) who, infuriated by his long imprisonment, has sworn to kill the person who releases him. The fisherman has to make a deal with the enraged jinni to survive—indeed, a devilish situation. The drawing depicts the Ifrit taking his monstrous form while the fisherman, on the ground far below, watches in dismay.

The story connected with the drawing used for the Three of Cups is captioned: "*Oh Lady, I am thy slave, thy Mameluke, thy white thrall, thy very bondsman.*" It is from "The Porter and the Three Ladies of Baghdad," a racy, erotic little tale. The porter, Hammal, is shown getting drunk with the three mysterious sisters in their luxurious hammam. However, the story involves the incredible secrets of the sisters, who demand of their visitors, "Speak not of what concerneth you not, lest ye hear what pleaseth you not." In some cases when the Three of Cups appears in a spread, the secrets that roil beneath the flow of social transactions can greatly influence both the actions and motivations of the participants. In this case, knowledge of the story would add greatly to the depth of possible card interpretations.

In a most dramatic merging of artwork and card meaning, the Ten of Swords depicts a man and a woman garbed in somber robes bowing over a tombstone in a lush garden. The drawing is captioned "*Nor from that time to this have I ceased to visit the tombs of Ali son of Bakkar and of Shams al-Nahar.*" The drawing illustrates the end of a tragic tale of star-crossed lovers who both die from the sorrow of their separation; the people looking over their tombs are Ali's friend, a jeweler, and Shams al-Nahar's faithful serving girl.

Several of the drawings are from the most famous tales in *The Arabian Nights* collection. The Ten of Pentacles (captioned "*And he lived with his wife in all solace and happiness*") is from the conclusion of "Alaeddin; or, the Wonderful Lamp." The Ten of Wands (captioned "*Suddenly the island shook and sank into the abysses of the deep*") is from "The First Voyage of Sinbad," while the Danger (the Tower) card's illustration, captioned "*The valley swarmed with*

The Ten of Swords from *Tarot of the Thousand and One Nights*

The Five of Wands from *Tarot of the Thousand and One Nights*

snakes and vipers, each as big as a palm tree," is from "The Second Voyage of Sinbad the Seaman."

The Five of Wands depicts a woman dancing in front of two men and a boy. This particular rendering seems odd for such a feisty tarot card. The illustration is from a segment of the very lengthy tale, "Ali Baba and the Forty Thieves," and is captioned *"Morgiana rose up and showed her perfect art."* Although it captures a moment of enjoyable after-dinner entertainment, Morgiana is using her dance to distract the dinner guest, who is actually the Master of the Robbers in disguise. Clever Morgiana whips out a dagger and stabs the man, thus saving Ali's life. The story line does somewhat fit the often dangerous Five of Wands, but the reader may be at a loss to interpret the drawing without knowing what the dancer is about to do.

The intricate designs of Carré's illustrations gush with luscious colors, rich ornamentation, and arabesques in the style of Persian carpets and the elaborate tile work featured in the architecture of the legendary city of Isphahan. The designs on walls, carpets, and tapestries, displayed to great effect in both the King and Queen of Chalices, reflect the organic and sinuous Persian style, adopted as an artistic outlet in a society prohibited by the tenets of Islam from portraying real-life subjects. Carré had no such prohibition, and he gave splendid life to the characters of *The Arabian Nights*. He particularly excels in depicting unusual or elderly men in his drawings; women are somewhat less differentiated and individualized.

The artist indulged in creating elaborate settings for the literary adventurers. Several cards depict palatial grandeur. Yet private lounges, hammam baths, and small cubbies are also featured, taking the observer from the gaudy luxury of royal palaces to the squalor of the poorest and humblest subjects. Exterior scenes explode with exotic flora and fauna, depicting well-tended garden pavilions and gardens with fountains, as well as pastoral meadows and woodland scenes. Other scenes are more panoramic, and it is here that Carré's color palette is at its finest. In both the Lovers and the Three of Wands, the twilit sky in the background is a radiant yet delicate rainbow of sky hues.

Carré also takes the unusual artistic challenging of showing overhead views of cities. These are featured in the Two of Wands, the Nine of Cups, and the Knight of Swords, and vault the reader into an unexpected viewpoint. These cityscapes give an intricate wealth of detail in depicting Persian architecture in its most exalted and idealized state. Some cards depict water or ocean scenes. Carré portrays the sea with almost impressionistic calm in the Six of Swords, and with crashing fury in the Eight of Chalices.

One of the most delightful features of *The Arabian Nights* is its cornucopia of magical creatures, and Carré doesn't stint on these, either. A female jinni manifests in front of a frightened man in the Seven of Cups, where the Devil card (previously mentioned) features an evil Ifrit-jinni. Mer-people are shown on the Ace of Chalices and the Seven of Wands. The Danger (Tower) and the Courage (Strength) cards show enormous vipers. A vampire or possessed woman races through a graveyard under a full moon on the Death card.

The Arabian Nights includes stories with angels—creatures who are much busier in these tales and in the Koran than in the Bible. The Judgement and Temperance cards both feature benevolent angelic figures, while the Nine of Swords shows a terrifying, dark, winged demon carrying away a defenseless maiden from her bed. The interaction between humans and supernatural beings and creatures amplifies the magical feel of this deck.

The Tarot of the Thousand and One Nights is a delight for any tarotist who adores the orientale idiom and work from the "Golden Age" of illustration art. Carré's obscurity is remarkable in the face of his efforts in the orientale style, which is popular with period collectors. My delight with this deck would have been even greater if the cards were bigger. The ornamental frames, while adding to the beauty of the deck, take away much-needed space from the pictures. Rather than sacrificing the lovely frames, I'd rather the deck was one-half to three-quarters of an inch bigger in both dimensions so I could see the pictures more clearly! Compared to the Franklin edition, the

The Knight of Swords from *Tarot of the Thousand and One Nights*

reproductions in the deck are incredibly crisp and clean, but it takes extremely keen eyes (or a magnifying glass) to distinguish Carré's intricate details in such tiny proportions.

The lack of information about the artwork is a serious omission. The stories behind the pictures that I was able to identify added a full harvest of meanings to the cards. The LWB just doesn't do the job it needs to do for this particular deck, and the resources for repairing this omission aren't available in North America (unless someone has the entire twelve-volume set in a private collection). The exquisite renderings cry for at least a little explanation. At some point I hope a separate volume to explain the deck becomes available, although to date Lo Scarabeo doesn't seem to have that priority in their publishing efforts.

This deck is highly recommended, in spite of the above remarks, for tarotists who are big fans of early twentieth-century illustration art. For those who are interested, search the art.com database to compare with Dulac's illustrations. While Dulac's luscious work is more accessible and well-known, Carré gains my heartfelt gratitude for the many years of effort he dedicated to these fabulous illustrations. And Lo Scarabeo deserves credit for recognizing Carré's magnum opus and assembling this substantial body of art work into a tarot deck.

Special thanks to librarian Andre Criner of Toledo-Lucas County Public Library for his assistance with research materials for this article.

The Sacred Circle Tarot

reviewed by Dallas Jennifer Cobb

L et go of the everyday, ordinary, and mundane. Allow yourself to move into the realm of the magical and mystical with the *Sacred Circle Tarot* as your guide. Let time become fluid as ancient merges with modern, and is digitally altered to return to the realm of the timeless and eternal.

How often do we get lost in the details of daily life and lose sight of the spiritual path and the roots of age-old wisdom? We forget that we are spiritual beings having a human experience when the demands of bills, obligations, and responsibilities overwhelm us.

But tools like the *Sacred Circle Tarot* can guide us back on track, affirming the deeper spiritual nature of our lives. The sacred images contained in the *Sacred Circle Tarot* will stimulate deeper symbolic identification and contemplation; the photographs and vivid colors will inspire and excite you; and the ancient meanings translated through the book portion of the deck will enliven and inform.

This is just the sort of tool to use to get up and out of the funk of everyday, whether you undertake a deep journey inside and redirect your life back to the spiritual realm, or you use it daily as a meditation tool to focus and calm the spirit.

As you slide into the *Sacred Circle Tarot* deck and the accompanying book, you will take a profound journey, awakening consciousness, moving through initiation and ultimately toward enlightenment. And you will become more aware of the infinite at work in your everyday life, and welcome the daily miracles and acts of magic that are all part of the rich, woven fabric of a spiritual life.

The circle of the title represents the many places and meanings of the circle as it exists in spiritual practices: the wheel of the year, the sacred circles of the landscape, casting sacred circles for ritual use, and the cyclical nature of life in the emotional, physical, and spiritual realms.

The Book

The book accompanying the *Sacred Circle Tarot* is rich with detail and information, including a concise historical overview of the spiritual settlement, invasion, and development of the British Isles. There is information about the major icons, images, symbols, and sacred objects and sites common to each wave of spiritual development throughout the ages. The depth and clarity embodied in the concise historical section is astounding: detailed origins of many of the Pagan symbols we commonly use and take for granted, with a short history lesson on their meaning.

The deck is organized to depict the Fool's Journey, a metaphor for the spiritual journey each of us takes toward consciousness. Every profound spiritual journey starts with our identification with the Fool and the admission that we know nothing. Only then is the journey started, and we can move toward consciousness.

Imagination

The Queen of Swords from the *Sacred Circle Tarot*

Queen of Swords

Moving through the *Sacred Circle*'s Major Arcana cards, renumbered from zero to twenty-two, a symbolic journey is taken as the initiate moves toward consciousness and enlightenment.

Starting with the Awakening cycle, the journey takes us through a dissolution of the old Self and into the initiation cycle. After many trials and tribulations, lessons and learning the initiate emerges into consciousness. The author outlines her vision of this journey in the introduction, and identifies the meaning imbued in each of the cards of the Major Arcana.

The Deck

A seventy-eight–card deck, the *Sacred Circle Tarot* deck has twenty-two Major Arcana cards like most other decks. The Minor Arcana consists of the four usual suits, which represent the four magical weapons of the four directions of the Tuatha De Danaan. Representing the east is the sword of Nuadha, which has become the suit of Swords. It symbolizes air, spirit, intellect, and the power of thought, and the season of spring from Imbolc to Beltane Eve. In the south is the spear of Lugh, which has become the suit of Wands or Rods, representing fierce spirit, creativity, and vision, and the summer season from Beltane to Lughnasa Eve. In the west is the cauldron of the Dagda, which has been transformed into the suit of Cups. It symbolizes water, emotion, psychic abilities, and autumn from Lughnasa to Samhain Eve. The last suit is characterized by the stone of Fal, which became Discs and later Pentacles. It represents the north, the physical realm, material possessions, and winter, from Samhain to Imbolc Eve.

Thought

Page of Swords

The Page of Swords from the *Sacred Circle Tarot*

While many of us use divination tools for everyday guidance and focus, this deck lends itself to the task of guiding us back to the larger spiritual journey that we take through the course of our lives. It uses images and icons that push us deeper into our own true meaning, and the path the deck outlines, which guides us through the commonly faced tests, trials, and tribulations that arise in the life of spiritual growth and evolution.

The Images

The *Sacred Circle Tarot* is a modern deck with ancient roots—literally and figuratively. In the literal sense, the deck relies on images that are based on traditional Pagan and mythological symbols from the British Isles. Refreshingly, the images do not draw on the Kabbalistic or Christian iconography that has crept into many modern tarot-deck images. Figuratively, the deck was conceived of a long time ago by the author and illustrator, and is only now coming into existence.

The Lady

3

The Lady from the Sacred Circle Tarot

Ironically, developments in modern technology and software have enabled the artists to produce their envisioned images and give birth to the deck. Produced using state-of-the-art computer technology, the imagery is a fantastic blend of photographs, digitally altered graphics, and paintings. The effect is magical and timeless, as images invoke deep feelings of remembrance and déjà vu.

Fifteen years in the making, this deck was conceived of and started long before it got produced. The author described her vision to the illustrator, who set about trying to produce images to match the text and meaning of the deck. Because the challenge was enormous, and the images didn't do justice to the ideas, the deck was shelved for fifteen years. It quite literally took that length of time for new media technology to catch up to the imagination of the creators.

With the development of computer-based photographic manipulation programs, the creators were able to easily collage, alter, and touch up the photographs that they took fifteen years earlier. The youthful images of the author and illustrator appear in the deck as well—the author as the Queen of Swords, the illustrator as the Page of Swords. The photos are symbolic of the journey that the two creators took: the Fool's journey. The Queen of Swords is also called Imagination, for she is the one who conceived of the idea for the deck. And the Page of Swords is also called Thought, for he is the one who had to figure out a means to bring the idea into being.

Combining photographs, pencil drawings, computer-generated graphics, and paintings, the images have been scanned, assembled in Photoshop, digitally altered and enhanced, and then filtered to produce light, tone, and shade effects. The overall effect is stunning. The cards convey a level of naturalism conducive to their theme and content, and inspire a deep sense of place.

While the deck is rooted in the British Pagan tradition, it remains accessible and interesting to a wider audience, particularly those who have roots in the British Isles.

A Bit About the British Pagan Teachings

Central to the British Pagan path is the theme of the land—not just as a symbol, but in a functional day-to-day relationship. The wheel of the seasons is observed and celebrated as Pagans immerse themselves in the ebb and flow of nature. Teachings are based on the land, embodied in the gods and goddesses, the animals, plants, and the wildfolk.

The history of the British Isles is one of mixing often disparate cultures and influences. Throughout repeated cycles of immigration, invasion, and inhabitation, the residents held fast to the spirit of the land, which did not change. And modern British Pagans have inherited the diverse images and influences from all of the ages and stages of British Pagan culture.

Each wave of invasion brought new images and spiritual practices, yet each was rooted in the land. The megalithic temples, standing stones, and burial chambers of the indigenous people of Britain, originating in the Neolithic period, attest to the prevalence of a cult of the dead, in which the cycles of the Sun and Moon were honored, reflecting the birth, life, death, and regeneration cycle central to the life they lived. The water cults of the Bronze Age (2200 to 1000 BCE.) inspired observance of the power and majesty of the ocean, rivers, streams, and lakes. Wells, lakes, and waterfalls were revered as sacred.

The Gaelic-speaking Celts arrived in Britain around 900 BCE and brought with them astronomical wisdom, Druids, and great festivals. The Roman invasions between 100 CE and 500 CE brought about a fusion between local deities and Roman deities. Heathen Saxons invaded after the withdrawal of the Romans (450 CE), followed by the Danes in 800 CE.

Almost all of these cultural influences predate the Christian invasion of the area, which started in 597 CE when many of the Pagan sites were built over with Christian churches, and wells were renamed after Christian saints. But throughout the period the ancient sacred sites remained sacred, and the sacred relationship with the land was central to spiritual practice. With the Viking invasion in the ninth century there was a quick reversion to Paganism because the populace hadn't really converted to Christianity, but merely made substitutions to preserve the icons and sacred sites of their faith.

The *Sacred Circle Tarot* brings us full cycle, drawing on all the images, icons, and symbols of all the invasions, connecting everything back to the sacred relationship with the land.

Working with the *Sacred Circle Tarot*

The authors of the book have provided six spreads for use with the deck: the twelve-card Zodiac Spread, the eight-card Circle Spread, the seven-card Planetary Spread, the twenty-one–card Romany Spread, the seventeen-card Web Spread, and the ten-card Celtic Cross Spread. Also included in the deck are cards depicting the lay-outs for the Planetary and Circle spreads.

After hours spent deeply enthralled with the book, I turned to the deck itself and started to work with the cards. Although the cards themselves were slightly too large for my hand—I was unable to easily hold them to shuffle—I managed to shuffle and energize the deck and then lay out a spread.

Initially I chose to do a reading based on my own knowledge of tarot cards and symbols, but found myself reaching for the accompanying deck because many of the symbols used weren't as familiar to me. Like driving a new car, I was aware of the difference in handling the deck. The lack of familiar imagery left me feeling uncertain. I wanted to put on the brakes. But then I started to enjoy the scenery, sinking into the gorgeous imagery unique to the deck and to the British Pagan tradition, and found myself pushing the pedal down so I could swoop and fly over ancient British land.

After touring the British Pagan countryside I was more aware of the confluence of modern Paganism and traditional British Paganism. My little British jaunt took me on the Fool's journey and renewed my conscious connection to the land and its spirit.

Pick up the *Sacred Circle Tarot* and take a journey to renew your connections, spirit, and joy. And while you are journeying, enjoy the lush scenery of these gorgeous cards.

The Witches Tarot

reviewed by Roslyn Reid

First published in 1989, *The Witches Tarot* by Ellen Cannon Reed is one of the best-loved tarot decks in use today. In fact, it was a good feeling to crack open my copy again for the purpose of this review. In my opinion, one cannot truly study the tarot by using only one deck. Why do I feel this way? Because *The Witches Tarot* was my second deck—the deck that opened my eyes to the many other possibilities of tarot reading.

Artwork

Personal disclosure: I love the vivid—almost lusty—artwork in this deck! Reed's brother, Martin Cannon, painted the pictures. Their three-dimensional imagery is much more vibrant than many other tarot decks, yet it is never a distraction like the art in some decks can be. Almost all of the people depicted in *The Witches Tarot* are good-looking; the colors are bright; and even the traditional "worst" card in the deck, the Tower, is beautiful. The deck's backing, a silver pentacle on a black background, is very soothing.

Originally the cards were borderless. However, in the latest edition, a black border has been added to each card, which makes quite an elegant frame for the pictures.

How Is This Deck Different?

The Witches Tarot departs from the *Rider-Waite-Smith* (RWS) standard in several respects. It still maintains the usual seventy-eight-card format: a twenty-two-card Major Arcana and the four suits of Cups, Wands, Pentacles, and Swords, with fourteen cards in each one (including four Court Cards).

Arthur Waite departed from the older tarot decks by switching the Major Arcana cards of Strength and Justice. In the *RWS* deck, Strength is VIII and Justice is IX. Strength remains in the same position in *The Witches Tarot*. However, Reed has inexplicably switched Justice with the Wheel of Fortune, resulting in Justice occupying the card X position and the Wheel of Fortune filling the XI slot. It's possible she may have been trying to establish a parallel between Justice and Judgement, card XX.

XV The Horned One

The Horned One from *The Witches Tarot*

Another major change Reed made was replacing the Devil with the Horned One. Many modern decks use an alternate image in this position because there is no single equivalent to the Devil in New Age or Pagan beliefs. However, I am ambivalent about this change. On the one hand, I really like the more positive image of the Horned One as a symbol of the earthly realm; on the other hand, I am concerned that some people—either maliciously or ignorantly—will use this substitution to equate the Horned One with the traditional Devil, when they are not at all related.

In other changes, the Hermit, card IX, has been replaced with the Seeker, who is holding his lantern aloft, letting his face be illuminated instead of trying to hide it. The generic Hanged Man usually found on card XII has been replaced with an image of Odin and his runes to better reflect the Pagan orientation of this deck. The Hierophant, card V, has been replaced by a High Priest performing the Ritual of the Cup and Sword. And as in a few other decks, the World, card XXI, has been replaced by the Universe.

Depicted as part of a sphere somewhere on each of the Major Arcana is one of the ten sephiroths, or lights, of the Kabbalistic Tree of Life. These do not appear on the Minor Arcana, which are full of typical Pagan symbolism. Because I'm not a student of it, the

Kabbalah aspect of the Major Arcana is probably my least favorite feature of *The Witches Tarot*. However, it seems to me that this deck can provide a good starting point for anyone who wishes to learn about the Kabbalah. The companion book, also called *The Witches Tarot*, provides all the necessary Kabbalistic correspondences, so even people who are more familiar with the Kabbalah can feel comfortable using this deck. Further information on the Kabbalah can be found in one of Reed's other books, *The Goddess and the Tree*.

The Minor Arcana

As stated, the Minor Arcana consists of the usual four suits of fourteen cards each. However, Reed made a couple of changes in the Court Cards: she replaced the customary Pages with Princesses, and Knights with Princes. Also, unlike the *RWS* deck, all the poses in the court cards are the same: the Princesses all have their eyes closed, the Kings are all standing and facing forward, etc. What is different in each suit is the color of the person's clothes, the accessories they are holding (wands, cups, etc.), and the settings in which they appear.

Much of the artwork in the Minors is quite striking. The depiction of the Cups—not so much vessels of liquid as of light—is stunning. The beauty of the Six and Seven of Cups is particularly breathtaking. Pentacles are typically solid and dependable . . . except for the Three—what a party! Wands are all over the creative map, from mystical to intriguing. Swords are appropriately powerful and dynamic.

Swords deserve a special mention here. As we know, each card in the tarot carries both positive and negative aspects. However, many readers feel that it is traditional to interpret Swords in a negative light. True, some of the Swords seem to depict particularly unfortunate events. However, it's obvious that *The Witches Tarot* prefers to lean toward the more positive side.

Take as an example the Ten of Swords. The *RWS* deck depicts it as a dead man with ten swords protruding from his back under a black sky. What could be positive about that? However, in *The Witches Tarot*, the picture shows a swordsman standing over a dead man and brandishing two swords in the air, while behind him a woman

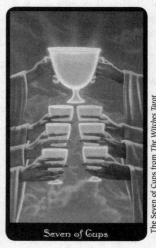

Seven of Cups

The Seven of Cups from *The Witches Tarot*

Ten of Swords

The Ten of Swords from *The Witches Tarot*

breaks free of her bonds. The other eight swords are scattered all over the ground. Here Reed has offered readers the choice of determining which figure best represents the client: is it the swordsman, the dead man, or the freed woman? Now, instead of being a card of doom, the Ten of Swords can be interpreted more positively because the swordsman appears to have liberated the woman rather than just inexplicably killing a man.

The Last Word

Who says art can't be utilitarian? The good news is that, like a beautiful thoroughbred, this deck is also a great workhorse. In fact, one of the main reasons I like *The Witches Tarot* is its virtual indestructibility, which is illustrated by the following story.

Years ago, one of my relatives became entangled with the wrong man. She was also a tarot reader, but felt that she could not read for herself. So she frequently asked me to do readings for her—all of them about him. Unfortunately, I found that whenever I used my *RWS* deck for her readings, she would second-guess me with interpretations she liked better (i.e., what she wanted to hear), or insist on a do-over because the answer "made no sense." As you can imagine, this had quite a chilling effect on the readings: the cards just repeated themselves, offering wimpier answers each time the same question was asked.

When I had eventually had enough of her interference, I broke out my *Witches Tarot*. It was immediately apparent that this deck was not about to absorb any of her negative energy. It stood up quite nicely to her repeated assertions that my interpretations were on the wrong track. *The Witches Tarot* told it like it was—the indications were quite clear (to me) that this man was really not very interested in her. And sure enough, later on he walked right out of her life.

If Ellen Cannon Reed is in Seventh Heaven right now, offering up tarot readings to Osiris, she can justifiably be proud of her masterpiece tarot deck. It will serve us well for many years to come.